SELECTS

BASEBALL'S GREATEST MOMENTS

Writer, Editorial Director

Ron Smith

ACKNOWLEDGEMENTS

The quality of any book is a reflection of the people who put it together. This project is the result of dedication and contributions from talented people at *The Sporting News*, many of whom provided valuable insight and assistance in addition to their regular weekly obligations.

The point man was executive editor Steve Meyerhoff, who directed the project through its planning stage, helped devise marketing strategies and assisted on the editing and writing process. Albert Dickson, TSN's chief photographer, accepted the challenge of finding and procuring the special photographs that appear in this book and prepress specialist David Brickey spent long hours making sure those photographs looked as good as they possibly could.

The design was conceptualized and executed by creative director Bill Wilson, who got assists from graphics specialists Amy Beadle and Christen Webster. Brickey received assistance from prepress director Bob Parajon and specialists Jack Kruyne, Steve Romer and Vern Kasal.

Editorial contributions were made by Dave Sloan, Michael Knisley and Bill Ladson. Sloan, an associate editor, provided proofreading and editing assistance while senior writer Knisley wrote the text for the Mark McGwire, Cal Ripken and Kirk Gibson moments. Associate editor Ladson wrote the Reggie Jackson chapter.

CONTENTS

1
THE SHOT HEARD 'ROUND THE WORLD
Page 10

4
FISK WAVES IT FAIR
Page 34

7
62 AND BEYOND
Page 52

2
MAZ
Page 20

5
HAMMERIN' HANK & THE BABE
Page 40

8
E-3
Page 60

3
LARSEN'S PERFECT GAME
Page 28

6
GIBSON DELIVERS IN A PINCH
Page 46

9
THE CATCH
Page 66

FOREWORD

by JOE MORGAN

When I received the list of Baseball's 25 Greatest Moments, my first thought was: "What a great list!"

I started at the top, with Bobby Thomson's Shot Heard 'Round the World. My mind raced back to all that I had heard and to all that I had read about the 1951 season and how baseball arrived with Thomson's great moment. The Giants had been 13½ games behind the Dodgers with 49 games to go. But they ultimately caught the Dodgers and Thomson took center stage in that playoff game. I can still hear the call: "The Giants win the pennant! The Giants win the pennant! The Giants win the pennant! ..."

A footnote to remember: The great Willie Mays was on deck when Thomson hit that home run. Willie told me he thought the manager, Leo Durocher, would have pinch hit for him because he was a rookie. Leo Durocher said, no, he would never have pinch hit for Mays. We'll never know for sure.

I then jumped to Moment No. 5: Hank Aaron's record-breaking home run. My first thought was of the hate mail and the animosity Hank had to endure chasing the most hallowed record in the game. Then I thought of Opening Day 1974 at Cincinnati, when I was at second base and Hank hit No. 714 off Jack Billingham. I remember nodding to Hank as he trotted past me at second base. What a fantastic moment for baseball and for me!

One of my personal favorites is the home run by Bill Mazeroski, a fellow second baseman, that won the 1960 World Series and beat the mighty Yankees. Even this great moment has a footnote: Maz's home run was only possible because of a

bad-hop single. Bill Virdon's ground ball had hopped up and hit Tony Kubek in the throat. That helped the Pirates turn a 7-4 eighth-inning Yankees lead into a 9-7 Pirates lead. The Yankees tied it in the ninth, only to lose it on Maz's great moment. The image of Mazeroski circling the bases with his hat held high above his head will always remind me that it is not always the biggest stars who do big things in big games.

My least favorite moment on the list is No. 4, Carlton Fisk's 12th-inning home run to win Game 6 of the 1975 World Series. In what may be the greatest game in the greatest World Series ever played, my view of Fisk's home run, from my second base position on the Fenway Park diamond, was different from what people saw on television. When Fisk first hit the ball, I immediately thought, "Home run. Game over. Drive safely." Then I saw him standing at home plate trying to wave it into fair territory and I thought it was going foul. When it hit the foul pole, I waited at second base. I tell people it was to make sure he touched the bag, but I really think I was in shock.

Fisk's home run was possible because Bernie Carbo hit a three-run, pinch-hit homer in the eighth to tie the score. It was possible because Dwight Evans robbed me of a homer in the top half of the 11th.

And that's why I love this list: It makes you think of more than just the moment itself. When you think of your favorite moments on this list, think of what preceded these great accomplishments, think of where you were sitting when you watched, read or heard about them.

If you are truly a baseball fan, you will remember.

Joe Morgan

One night after Fisk hit his Game 6 home run in 1975, Morgan delivered a World Series-deciding single in the ninth inning off this pitch from Boston lefty Jim Burton.

INTRODUCTION

Maybe our idea of a "Greatest Moment" is restrictive, but the very nature of this collection, the very definition of the word "moment," demands that.

We're not dealing here with historical significance. We're not promoting career, single-season or single-game accomplishments. We're looking for pure, unadulterated, instant gratification.

A "Greatest Moment" comes from edge-of-your-seat intensity, the do-or-die, nail-biting situations that arise most often in World Series, playoffs or other meaningful games. Bill Mazeroski's home run brought a stunning conclusion to the 1960 World Series. Bobby Thomson's home run brought shocking closure to one of the great pennant races in baseball history. Willie McCovey, facing Yankees righthander Ralph Terry with runners at second and third, two out in the bottom of the ninth inning and the Giants trailing 1-0 in Game 7 of the 1962 World Series, hit a vicious line drive, but right at second baseman Bobby Richardson. That was the epitome of dramatic.

A "Greatest Moment" results from an amazing, out-of-the-blue, unexpected development that almost knocks the viewer out of his chair. Kirk Gibson, barely able to stand, much less swing the bat, connects off Dennis Eckersley for a game-winning World Series homer. Mickey Owen's passed ball on a swinging third strike that would have ended a World Series game triggers an incredible Yankees comeback victory. Bill Buckner commits baseball's most infamous World Series error.

A "Greatest Moment" comes from the culmination of a record-setting chase or a heart-wrenching development. Hank Aaron's 715th home run had a lot of drama, even though everybody knew it was inevitable. So did Pete Rose's 4,192nd hit and Cal Ripken's Iron Man celebration. Lou Gehrig's "Luckiest Man Alive" speech qualifies, as does the joy that enveloped Brooklyn—finally—with the last pitch of the 1955 World Series.

A "Greatest Moment" floods your mind with memories and makes you remember where you were or what you were doing at the time. The sheer memory generates the same goosebumps and spine-tingling sensation it made you feel when you watched it or read about it for the first time. Does it make you shake your head in amazement every time you think about it? Does it withstand the test of time as new "moments" pile up? Can you remember the key and peripheral characters involved?

A "Greatest Moment" is not:

■ An event that looms big in history for obvious reasons, but doesn't pass any of the above tests.

■ A contrived event or non-event that has lived on in baseball mythology.

■ A play within the course of a memorable game.

Surely, we can rattle off a list of baseball's great accomplishments, many by some of the game's greatest stars—Joe DiMaggio's 56-game hitting streak, Nolan Ryan's 5,000 strikeouts, Babe Ruth's 60 home runs in 1927—but they are not great "moments." That doesn't diminish their significance or their lasting place in baseball history.

Momentous? Yes. Moments? No.

Dozens passed our test; hundreds did not. Twenty-five (plus a few more) captured our collective attention.

LOU. GEHRIG
Nº 4

Hartung down the line at third, not taking any chances. Lockman without too big of a lead at second—but he'll be running like the wind if Thomson hits one. Branca throws ... There's a long drive! It's going to be, I believe ...! The Giants win the pennant! The Giants win the pennant! The Giants win the pennant! The Giants win the pennant! Bobby Thomson hits into the lower deck of the left field stands! The Giants win the pennant! And they're going crazy! They're going crazy! Oh ho!
—Russ Hodges, October 3, 1951

THE SHOT HEARD 'ROUND THE WORLD

I t was a bolt of lightning, an electrifying streak that lit up the baseball world with its shocking impact. But almost a half-century later, all that remains of "The Shot Heard 'Round the World" is grainy newsreel footage of Bobby Thomson dancing triumphantly around the bases, a jubilant Eddie Stanky jumping on Leo Durocher's back near third base and the Giants celebrating euphorically in a mob scene near home plate at New York's Polo Grounds.

And the memory.

The memory of radio announcer Russ Hodges' historic call when Thomson

THE SHOT HEARD 'ROUND THE WORLD

drove Brooklyn righthander Ralph Branca's second pitch into the lower left field stands: "The Giants win the pennant! The Giants win the pennant! The Giants win the pennant! ..."

"I think that will always be in the minds of the ballplayers the greatest moment in sports history," says former shortstop Alvin Dark, a .303 hitter for the 1951 Giants. "To us, it was that one big game and nothing has ever happened to equal that."

To fully appreciate the dent Thomson made in America's baseball psyche, it's necessary to rewind the 1951 season to August 11, the day the Dodgers won the opener of a doubleheader from the Boston Braves, thereby lifting their N.L. lead to a whopping $13^1/_2$ games over the struggling Giants. The hated Giants.

"When you had (Chuck) Dressen and Leo (Durocher) managing against each other, it was dog eat dog," says former Giants right fielder Don Mueller. "It was kind of mean."

"How I hated (the Dodgers) then," recalled Thomson in 1963. "Really hated them. Leo Durocher instilled that in us. But I must say the papers played their part, too, in drumming up the rivalry. If you played for Leo, the whole world was right if you beat the Dodgers. Nothing else mattered."

It was with such emotional fervor that the Giants pulled off a three-game Polo Grounds sweep of the Dodgers shortly after that August 11 low, cutting their deficit to $9^1/_2$ games and launching an amazing comeback that would become known as "The Miracle at Coogan's Bluff."

"I had the best seat in the house—the best view. Had the ball been hit in Ebbets Field, I might have had a shot at it. But in the Polo Grounds, it was only 279 feet down the line. It was about 20 feet off the line and it landed in the fourth or fifth row. When it left the bat, I thought I might have a chance to catch it."

Dodgers left fielder Andy Pafko

A 16-game win streak trimmed the Dodgers' lead to 5 and a stunning stretch-run combination of Giants victories and Dodgers defeats left the teams deadlocked for first place with two games remaining. Both teams won out, Brooklyn barely surviving in the finale when Jackie Robinson beat the Philadelphia Phillies with a 14th-inning home run.

The Giants, who had wiped out a $4^1/_2$-game deficit with seven games remaining, finished the regular season with a 37-7 run, victories in 12 of their last 13 games and a 96-58 record. And they opened a three-game pennant playoff at Brooklyn's Ebbets Field with a 3-1 victory, thanks to home runs by Thomson and Monte Irvin. When the Dodgers fought back with a 10-0 win at the Polo Grounds behind the six-hit pitching of Clem Labine and home runs by Robinson, Gil Hodges, Andy Pafko and Rube Walker, the scene was set for a winner-take-all showdown.

The October 3 clincher developed into a pitching duel between Giants right-hander Sal Maglie and Brooklyn ace Don

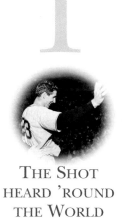

1

THE SHOT HEARD 'ROUND THE WORLD

Thomson pulled his dramatic home run to left field, where Pafko watched it disappear into the crowd, directly over the 315-foot sign.

315 FT.

Giants players and coaches mob Thomson at home plate, a fitting celebration for one of the most stunning comeback stories in major league history.

While ecstatic fans demanded curtain calls, Giants (left to right) Thomson, winning pitcher Larry Jansen and Maglie whooped it up inside the clubhouse.

Newcombe. Thomson's seventh-inning sacrifice fly tied the game at 1-1, but the Dodgers finally got to Maglie for three runs in the eighth and Newcombe, seemingly in full control, carried a 4-1 lead into the bottom of the ninth.

"He (Newcombe) was great that day," Dark said. "And it was twilight time, a cloudy day. It just seemed dark. And he was still throwing the ball good."

Thomson recalled the helpless feeling as an incredible season neared an unhappy climax. "I never felt worse in my life than when I ran into the dugout for our last lick in the bottom of the ninth," he said. "I concluded that we weren't good enough, that we just couldn't make it, that it was hopeless."

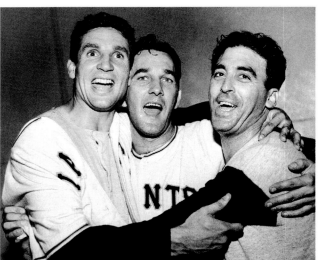

Thomson, a 28-year-old third baseman, perked up when Dark led off the ninth with an infield single and Mueller followed with a single to right, putting runners on first and third. Mueller's ground-ball hit would have been gobbled up by the slick-fielding Hodges if he had

A disconsolate Branca sits dejectedly on the clubhouse steps, feeling the pain of baseball's most celebrated home run.

"For about the first half-hour or so afterward, I guess I was the unhappiest guy in the world. I felt I'd let everybody down. But then somebody persuaded me to go in and take my shower and when I did, I began to feel better. ... I did what I was supposed to do. I kept the ball high——chin-high. He hit a chin-high fastball."

Dodgers pitcher Ralph Branca

not been holding Dark at first. When Irvin fouled out, the stage was set for Giants first baseman Whitey Lockman.

"I went up there with the idea of hitting a home run," Lockman told a reporter in 1974. "If I hit one out it would have tied the game. I'd always hit pretty well against Newcombe, so that's what I was going for. There was a short porch in right (257 feet down the line) and I was just looking for the right pitch. The first pitch was a fastball for a strike on the outside.

"Then muscle memory took over for me. I reached out and put (the next pitch) into left field instead. I knew it was

a base hit and figured one run was going to score anyway, perhaps two."

Pafko, the Dodgers' left fielder, played the ball well and fired to third base trying to nail Mueller. Mueller slid in safely on Lockman's double, but he jammed his foot, damaging the tendons in his ankle. In considerable pain, Mueller was transported on a stretcher to the Polo Grounds' center field clubhouse as Clint Hartung was summoned as the pinch-runner.

"Mueller's injury had a calming effect on all of us, breaking the tension," said Thomson, the Giants' next scheduled hitter.

While Mueller was being tended, Dressen phoned the Dodgers' bullpen, asking coach Clyde Sukeforth for an evaluation of Branca and Carl Erskine—the two pitchers available for relief duty. "Branca's popping the ball," Sukeforth reported. "Erskine's not at his best." Branca was brought in to face Thomson with first base open and rookie center fielder Willie Mays on deck.

What had appeared destined to be an ordinary Dodgers victory suddenly turned tense, with 34,320 sets of eyes focused squarely on Thomson and Branca. Dark, watching intently from the dugout, liked the matchup.

"What was in my mind was that Bobby Thomson, over the last $2^1/_2$ to 3 months of the season, was our best run-production hitter," he said. "He drove in a lot of big runs. That was the thing going

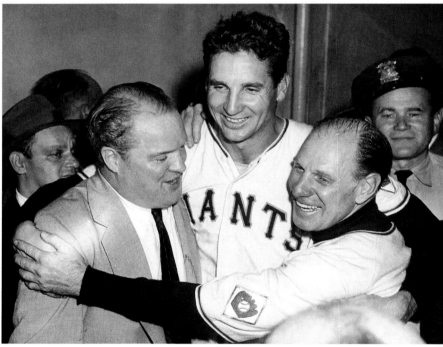
"We won't live
long enough to
see anything
like it again."

**Former Giants
pitcher
Carl Hubbell,
an observer
at the game**

through my mind. I had no idea he'd hit a home run. When you have runners on second and third and one out, your first thought is to get those two runners in, then go from there."

Branca's first pitch was a fastball right down the middle. Thomson froze, taking the pitch for strike one. Branca's second pitch also was a fastball, high and inside, just where he wanted it. Thomson pulled back, took a big cut and connected.

"If I'd been a good hitter, I'd have taken the damn ball," Thomson said later. "It was almost head high."

Branca couldn't believe what he was seeing.

"I'll never forget watching it head out toward left field," he said in a game account that appeared in THE SPORTING NEWS. "I thought it was just a long fly at first. I thought it was the second out and that one run was in. But then I saw he'd pulled it more than I'd thought he had. I knew then that it was going to hit the fence and that the score would be tied. But I kept praying that it wouldn't go in.

"And right up to the last second I didn't think it would. I can still see Pafko right up against the wall and I can hear myself saying, 'Sink, sink ... don't go over.' But it did and all I could do was to stuff my glove in my pocket and head for the clubhouse. The season was over and the pennant we had all wrapped up for weeks was gone.

"That walk across the field was the longest I've ever taken. I could hear the fans roaring and I knew the Giants were going crazy. I wished there was a hole in the ground that could have swallowed me up."

Even as the ball headed toward

baseball immortality, the Giants were not thinking home run.

"Our first thought was we're going to score those two, not having any idea the ball was going to go in the lower deck," Dark said. "That's the first ball that we'd ever seen go into the lower stands in left field. We had never seen that. The top bleachers in left field, the upper stands, stuck out over the bottom wall about 18 to 20 feet. We'd seen a lot of balls into left field hit the high left field wall or the stands in left, above the lower deck. But we had never seen one go into the lower deck."

Thomson is sandwiched by Giants owner Horace Stoneham (left) and Durocher after his pennant-deciding home run.

The ball found its home run window, just above the 315-foot sign as Pafko watched it land about five rows deep. There was a momentary hush as fans collected their thoughts—the calm before an incredible storm. Thomson, who finished his season with 32 homers and 101 RBIs, recalled his moment with dreamy amazement.

"'We beat 'em, we beat 'em,' I kept saying to myself as I loped around the bases," he said. "I felt like I was floating, like my feet weren't touching the ground. Rounding third, I had to fight Durocher off my back. Then I took a big jump on home plate and the next thing I knew everybody was whacking the tar out of me. I thought somebody was trying to tackle me, but it turned out to be Lockman lifting me on his shoulder."

Unsuccessfully.

"I'm at home plate and Thomson is stepping on the plate with a home run," Lockman recalled. "Everybody's going crazy and I figure Thomson's done such a great thing that I'll carry him off on my shoulders. I reach down and start to lift, but by this time about 8,000 fans are all around us and they're on me, too, and I went down for the count.

"I panicked a little because some of them were on me and I got a wrenched neck getting myself up and then we all raced to the clubhouse to drink champagne."

When the Giants reached the clubhouse, Mueller, laid out on a trainer's table, finally figured out what had happened.

"I didn't see it. I didn't hear it on the radio," he said. "All I heard was the crowd roar and the game was so close to being over I didn't know who had won. I didn't know until the team started coming into the clubhouse. They were so full of pep.

"Up to that point, all I had was the roar of the crowd. There were probably as many Dodger fans there as there were Giants fans, so you couldn't tell by that."

Safely in the clubhouse, Thomson retired to a corner, sick to his stomach and gasping for air. Hundreds of fans stood at the bottom of the clubhouse steps, chanting and calling for players, who appeased them with numerous curtain calls.

"The fans were at the bottom of our steps," Dark said. "They were down there around those steps hollering to the players. I don't know how long that lasted, but our first thought was, 'Hey, we've got a game tomorrow in the World Series at Yankee Stadium—a day game—and we gotta get to bed.' "

The Dodgers' clubhouse was like a morgue—so quiet you could hear a dream drop. Branca, in full uniform, sprawled face down across the steps dividing the two-level dressing area, his feet on the floor and his head buried in his arms on the top step. Tears flowed as players searched for answers that would never come.

Should the Dodgers have walked the hot-hitting Thomson, who already had two hits in the game, and pitched to the rookie Mays, a .274 season hitter who was having a bad playoff series? If Hodges hadn't been holding Dark in the ninth, could the Dodgers have turned a double play on Mueller's ground ball? Was Thomson's shot, on a bad pitch he normally wouldn't be able to hit, a simple case of destiny?

Thomson, an instant New York celebrity, appeared on the Perry Como Show the night of his home run. But the Giants went on to drop a six-game World Series to the Yankees. That, however, did not tarnish the moment that became one of the enduring reference points in sports history.

"After the season we had," Lockman said, "even the World Series was an anticlimax."

Thomson, a Scotsman, was an instant hero throughout New York and a guest on the Perry Como Show (with Maglie, bottom photo) after his dramatic home run.

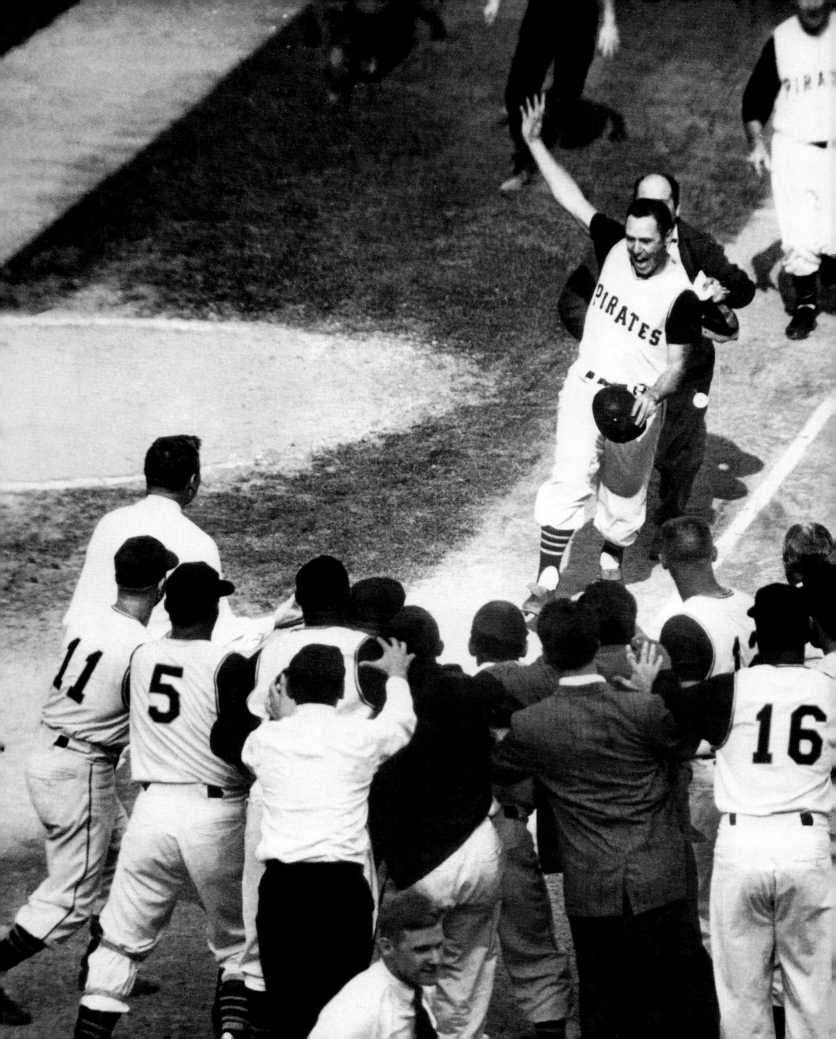

—CHUCK THOMPSON, OCTOBER 13, 1960

MAZ

It was not your average, everyday home run. When Pittsburgh second baseman Bill Mazeroski drove a belt-high slider over the left field wall at Forbes Field and brought a shocking end to another season, the baseball world stood still. Not only did Mazeroski fulfill the fantasy of every wannabe sports hero, he provided a dramatic memory that would last forever and a time reference for a generation of baseball-hungry Americans.

October 13, 1960.

"Most of the people tell me they won money on my homer or they lost money on it," Mazeroski said in a 1970 edition of THE SPORTING NEWS. "People tell me where they were when I hit the homer. Most of

BASEBALL'S
25 GREATEST
MOMENTS

21

OFFICIAL WATCH

LONGINES

AMERICAN			
P RP		1 2 3 4 5 6 7 8 9 10	H

BATTER
9

BALL STRIKE
1

OUT

UMPIRES

1ST 2ND 3RD
HOME PLATE

NATIONAL			
P RP		1 2 3 4 5 6 7 8 9 10	H
1 9 23	N.YORK	0 0 0 0 1 4 0 2 2	2
3 2 3 1	PITTS.	2 2 0 0 0 0 0 5	

SCORE CARD

NEXT GAME HERE PITTSBURGH

SCORE CARD

The scoreboard tells a dramatic story as Mazeroski sends his World Series-ending home run toward the left field fence at Pittsburgh's Forbes Field.

the fellows say they were working or in a bar watching the game on television. The women tell me what they were cooking that day, or where they were sitting."

Something special was brewing from the moment the Pirates and New York Yankees arrived at Forbes Field for the seventh game of an unusual World Series. The powerful and heavily-favored New Yorkers, who had won eight Fall Classics over a 13-year span, had posted wins by the lopsided scores of 16-3, 10-0 and 12-0. The Pirates, looking for their first championship in 35 years, had prevailed 6-4, 3-2 and 5-2. The Yankees entered the finale with striking edges in hits (78-49), runs (46-17) and average (.341-.241). The

Pirates entered Game 7 with a sense of destiny.

"When we talk about 1960, winning the Series was the highlight, there's no question about that," recalls Pirates center fielder Bill Virdon. "But when we look back, if you look for times in your career that you remember, I don't just remember the Series. I remember the year 1960. It seemed like from Day One everything happened right. Any time we needed a run, any time we needed an out, any time we needed something to happen to win, it happened. Somebody was on our side.

"I really, sincerely believe the Yankees had a better club than we did, overall talent. But I didn't consider they were more capable of winning just because of the nature of our club. The club never gave up, and everybody was very capable of doing the job they had to do. And it just seems like things happened."

Game 7 provided a microcosm of that destiny. The Pirates struck early against Yankees starter Bob Turley and reliever Bill Stafford, building a 4-0 lead on first baseman Rocky Nelson's two-run homer and Virdon's two-run single. But the Yankees fought back against Vernon Law with a single run in the fifth on first baseman Bill Skowron's opposite-field homer and four more in the sixth, three coming on a home run by Yogi Berra. Two more runs in the eighth extended the New York lead to 7-4 and set the stage for a stunning Pittsburgh rally.

The Pirates' big eighth inning was set up by Virdon's routine ground ball to shortstop Tony Kubek, after pinch-hitter Gino Cimoli had singled to open the inning.

"It was a routine double-play ball, no question about it," Virdon recalled. "In the eighth inning, with a three-run deficit, your chances of winning are pretty slim. But with that break, we scored five runs. I think we were supposed to win."

"That break" was a reference to the nasty hop the ball took off the hard infield, striking Kubek in the throat and knocking him down. Both runners were safe, Kubek was removed from the game and sent to the hospital for overnight treatment. He could barely speak the next day, courtesy of a bruised larynx.

"I didn't have a chance on the play," Kubek whispered to a reporter the next day. "I went down to pick up what looked like a double-play ball and then suddenly the ball came up and struck me in the

Berra watches Mazeroski's home run disappear into the trees beyond the left field wall.

neck. It happened so quickly that I couldn't even raise my glove in self-defense."

With the door slightly opened, shortstop Dick Groat singled home a run off reliever Bobby Shantz, who was replaced by Jim Coates. Two outs later, Roberto Clemente's infield single (the result of Coates failing to cover first base) scored another run, making the score 7-6 and setting the stage for backup catcher Hal Smith. Yankees manager Casey Stengel ambled out to the mound, conferred with his pitcher and then ambled back to the dugout. Moments later Stengel watched Smith, a defensive replacement in the top of the inning, belt a Coates pitch over the left field fence. The journeyman catcher literally danced home with the run that gave Pittsburgh a shocking 9-7 advantage.

"The Pirates should never have beaten our club," said an emotional Roger Maris after the game. "I think if we played them all season, we'd beat them real bad. They were real lucky. I think it's impossible for them to get any more breaks than they had in this Series."

The Yankees got a break of their own during a two-run ninth-inning rally that tied the game. Second baseman Bobby Richardson and pinch-hitter Dale Long singled to open the ninth off Bob Friend, who failed to retire a batter in his unusual relief role. Harvey Haddix came on to retire Maris on a foul pop, but Mickey Mantle singled home Richardson and sent Long to third, where he was replaced by Gil McDougald. The Series hung by a thread when Berra rocketed a shot that Nelson fielded, stepping on first base.

Nelson, looking for a Series-ending double play, looked toward second and was surprised to see Mantle only a few feet

2

MAZ

"Yes, it was a big break for us when Bill Virdon's ball took that bad hop and hit Tony Kubek. But I can't say I'm surprised at what followed. We've come from so far back so often that nothing surprises me any more."

Pirates manager
Danny Murtaugh

off first base. As McDougald dashed for the plate, Mantle dived for the bag, barely avoiding Nelson's lunging tag. McDougald scored, tying the game 9-9.

"He would not have reached home plate by the time Mantle was tagged," Richardson recalls. "It goes down as a great play (by Mantle), but it really wasn't a good play. Everybody said what a good baserunning play it was, but really he should have got caught in a rundown. That would have given McDougald plenty of time to cross the plate. It was an instinctive move and (Mickey) probably felt he could get back in and, of course, he did."

And he set up Mazeroski, a slick-fielding, light-hitting second baseman, for the first World Series-ending home run in the history of the Fall Classic. Yankees righthander Ralph Terry, who had come on to retire Don Hoak for the final out in the eighth, remembers the moment well.

"I was just trying to make good pitches," he recalls. "Down-and-away breaking pitches. I threw a slider and it was high. (Catcher John) Blanchard called time and came out to the mound and told me I have to get the ball down, that Mazeroski's a pull hitter. Well, I got the

second slider down, about belt high. He hit it good. I didn't think it was going to clear the fence. You've got to give him credit. It was one of the most dramatic home runs in the history of the game."

Terry and the Yankees dashed for the clubhouse as Maz took his arm-waving victory lap around the bases, Pittsburgh fans flooded the field and the Pirates celebrated wildly near the plate. Looking back after almost four decades, Terry accepts his victim role philosophically—and realistically.

"I hadn't relieved probably in a couple of months," he said. "I warmed up five times in that game, starting in the very first inning. After the second warmup, I

didn't have anything left. It was still in the bullpen. I was up and down all day. Usually, when you get up a couple of times and sit down, they switch to somebody else. But, the same thing was going on in their bullpen. Both pitching staffs were worn out.

"I didn't have much, I really didn't. Also I warmed up all day on this little bitty mound—a steep little mound. And then I get in the game on this big mound and everything I threw was high. I couldn't make the adjustment. I threw Don Hoak a hanging slider and he popped it up."

Terry was not so fortunate against Mazeroski.

"I'll never forget," he said, "when we went to take the field in the ninth Casey Stengel says, 'Go get 'em boys.' Two pitches later, we were walking off the field."

"As soon as he hit it, I had an idea it was gone," Richardson says. "Yogi was playing left field and when the ball was hit I just looked at him and I could tell it was out of the park. His expression was such you could tell there was no play on that."

2

MAZ

The two-page sequence relives Mazeroski's triumphant 1960 run around the bases—one of the most jubilant home run trots in baseball history.

MAZ

"The next spring I go to spring training and all the writers are asking, 'Is this going to warp you psychologically, this traumatic experience?' and I said, 'I'm 25 years old, I just pitched in my first World Series, I'm looking forward to a new season. We've got Mantle, Maris, Yogi and all these great players, we're going to get another shot at them. Why should it bother me?'"

Yankees righthander Ralph Terry

In the Pirates' dugout, hope quickly turned to ecstasy.

"We weren't sure," Virdon said. "From the flight of the ball we went to Berra and watched his reaction. We could tell he wasn't going to catch it. We knew we at least had a man on second with a good chance to win. But the ball just kept going and went out of the ballpark. My first feeling was relief."

The feelings were a lot harder to swallow in the Yankees' clubhouse.

"Mantle said that was his biggest disappointment—the '60 World Series," says Richardson, who earned MVP honors for his World Series-record 12-RBI performance. "It was mine, too. We felt like the best team had lost. That's because we had scored so many runs. We let some easy games slip by. Then, all of a sudden it was tied up. And we were thinking about a couple of plays. We had one play with two outs where the pitcher forgot to cover first. That would have taken us out of the (eighth) inning. And there was the play with Tony Kubek. It was a double-play ball."

While Richardson was lamenting what might have been, Terry was seeking solace for a pitch that forever would brand him as a goat in baseball's unforgiving history books.

"After the game, I went in and talked to Casey," Terry says. "I felt bad for Stengel, more than myself or anyone else. I loved Casey Stengel. He was a great inspirational manager to me. ... We pretty well knew it was his last year, so I really felt bad for Casey.

"I said, 'Casey, I really feel bad it ended this way.' He said, 'How were you trying to pitch to him?' I said, 'Breaking stuff, low and away, but I couldn't get the damn ball down.' He said, 'As long as you pitch, you're not always going to get the ball where you want to. That's a physical mistake. But if you went against the scouting report with high, hard stuff, then I wouldn't sleep good at night.' Then he said, 'Forget about it. Don't let it worry you.'

"And you know what? The Yankee fans are the greatest in the world. They never,

ever came down on me for that. They never held that against me. I never got any bad response from those people and I love those Yankee fans for that."

In retrospect, there are a lot of "what ifs" from the 1960 World Series that could have changed the course of baseball history. What if Mantle had been tagged out at first base in the ninth inning of Game 7? The Series would have been over and Mazeroski never would have batted. What if the ball had not taken a bad hop on Kubek? What if Coates had covered first

base on Clemente's hit? What if Stengel had started Whitey Ford in Game 1 instead of Art Ditmar, possibly making him available for a few innings in Game 7?

But destiny triumphed again.

"Do I think of that home run?" Mazeroski asked rhetorically when questioned by a reporter years after the defining moment of his career. "Every day of my life I think of that home run. Wouldn't you if you had hit it? People always are reminding me of it. I suppose it must be the most important thing I've ever done."

Pirates fans celebrate Mazeroski's homer from a rooftop overlooking Forbes Field (below). Front and center in a victorious clubhouse were Mazeroski (right, left photo) and manager Danny Murtaugh.

Two strikes and a ball ... Mitchell waiting, stands deep, feet close together. Larsen is ready, gets the sign. Two strikes, ball one. Here comes the pitch. Strike three! A no-hitter! A perfect game for Don Larsen!

—BOB WOLFF, OCTOBER 8, 1956

DON LARSEN'S PERFECT GAME

The image endures, more vivid even than the moment it represents. Yogi Berra, the man behind the mask, leaps joyously into the arms of a near-catatonic pitcher, wrapping powerful legs around his waist. Don Larsen, caught in Yogi's full-body squeeze, smiles broadly as teammates converge for a group hug. Chaos. Delirium.

The perfect end to a perfect game.

How ironic it seems more than four decades later that the only perfect pitching performance in World Series history was accomplished by one of the game's more imperfect players. Call it baseball irony: An unbelievable feat perpetrated by the most unlikely of characters in the most glamorous spotlight imaginable.

"Knowing Don, he was the last person

anybody would expect to pitch a perfect game," recalls former New York Yankees teammate Gil McDougald. "Before he came to (the Yankees), he was a losing pitcher. His record was poor. It's pretty hard when you haven't established yourself as a real good pitcher. But that's what happens sometimes."

Larsen, a 30-40 career pitcher entering the 1956 postseason, was better than "good" on that chilly fall afternoon, when he pitched the Yankees to a 2-0 victory over Brooklyn in Game 5 at Yankee Stadium, giving the New Yorkers a three-games-to-two Series edge. In the process, the enigmatic righthander retired all 27 Dodgers he faced, silenced critics of his sometimes erratic career and rewarded manager Casey Stengel for his unwavering patience.

The scoreboard (above), Berra's leap of joy into Larsen's arms and the ensuing celebration capture the essence of a perfect moment.

"He can be one of baseball's great pitchers any time he puts his mind to it," Stengel had insisted to reporters who questioned his decision to match the 27-year-old Larsen in a Series showdown against Dodgers righthander Sal Maglie, a big-game veteran. This was the same Larsen who had lost 21 games in 1954 while pitching for Baltimore, the same free spirit with a well-documented affinity for the New York night life. After a solid 11-5 regular season for the Yankees, Larsen had failed to survive the second inning of World Series Game 2, walking four batters and allowing four runs in an eventual 13-8 Yankee loss.

"That second game I started I had a 6-0 lead," Larsen recalls. "But I got wild and Casey never liked that. Nobody did. You have no chance to get anybody out."

True to form, Larsen was out—with a New York sportswriter the night before his Game 5 start. Reports circulated that Larsen returned to his hotel 10 minutes after his midnight curfew. Larsen admits he was out, but not as late as reported. "Arthur Richman and I were out," he says. "I had a low-key night and went to bed pretty early

after a couple of drinks. You know how those rumors start and get around."

Whatever his pregame routine, Larsen was ready when he took the mound in the first inning and began showing the Dodgers his unusually active repertoire of "fastballs, sliders and slow curves," all of which he threw with surgical precision under the direction of Berra, who had never seen Larsen work with such control and finesse.

"He was great," Berra would say after the game. "I've never caught a greater pitcher than Don was today."

Larsen, working from the no-windup delivery he had adopted late in the season to help his concentration, opened the game by striking out Jim Gilliam and Pee Wee Reese and retiring Duke Snider on a line drive to right fielder Hank Bauer. Reese went down on a full-count pitch, the only batter who would take Larsen to three balls during his 97-pitch masterpiece. The Dodgers' second inning opened when Jackie Robinson smashed a line drive that was deflected by third baseman Andy Carey to shortstop McDougald, who threw Robinson out at first.

"The ball they always talked about was

"I really didn't
even know he had
a no-hitter until
the eighth inning.
We were just
concentrating on
winning the ballgame."

Yankees left fielder
Enos Slaughter

the one Jackie Robinson hit that ricocheted off Andy Carey to me in the hole," McDougald says. "And they always asked me about that being a big play. And I said, 'That was only the second inning. How can it be a big play?' It just turned out that way."

After Robinson was retired, Larsen settled into a groove that took him through the fourth inning without incident. His fastball was painting the corner; his sliders and curves were breaking hard and true. "Control," Larsen says. "That was the difference. In Game 5, I threw the ball pretty close to where Yogi wanted it and when I made a mistake the defense took care of it."

Larsen's transformation was not lost on 64,519 Yankee Stadium fans, but Maglie, the Dodgers starter, was matching him pitch for pitch. The first nine Yankees went down without incident and Maglie set down Bauer and first baseman Joe Collins in the fourth. But Mickey Mantle broke the double no-hitter with a low line drive into the right field seats, just inside the foul pole.

Staked to a 1-0 lead, Larsen retired Robinson on a fly ball to open the fifth. But Dodgers first baseman Gil Hodges, a 32-homer man during the regular season, drove a pitch into deep left center field.

"Mantle made a beautiful catch," Larsen says. "That ball probably would have been a home run in most parks, but Yankee Stadium at that time was pretty big in left-center. Mantle could run like a deer, caught that ball and I had another sigh of relief."

But only temporarily. The next batter, Sandy Amoros, hit a long drive toward the right field corner, but the ball curved foul, preserving the lead and the no-hitter.

"When I saw that ball heading for the right field seats, I was ready to concede the homer," Bauer said after the game. "But when it hooked foul by this much, I was the happiest guy in the park." Bauer smiled broadly as he held his thumb and forefinger about three inches apart.

Frustrated Dodgers players agreed

Brooklyn owner Walter O'Malley, caught up in the moment, asked for an autograph after Larsen had shut down his Dodgers.

there was a fine line between success and failure in Larsen's bid to pitch baseball's first postseason no-hitter. They called it a simple case of bad timing.

"We were in the wrong ballpark," Maglie said, suggesting that Mantle's drive would have bounced off the high right field screen at Ebbets Field and Hodges' drive would have cleared the left-center field fence. "Mickey would have had to climb mighty high if he'd caught that one in Brooklyn," Hodges said.

Larsen breezed through the sixth and watched the Yankees extend the lead to 2-0 in the bottom of the inning when Bauer singled home Carey. An easy seventh suddenly raised the level of anticipation—and tension—among hardened fans who had witnessed six Yankee World Series championships and eight American League pennants since 1947.

"After the seventh inning, I came into the dugout and I was smoking a cigarette and I bumped into Mantle," Larsen recalls. "I told him, 'Look at the scoreboard. Wouldn't it be something. Two more innings to go.' He didn't say anything. He just walked away from me.

"Then it got like a morgue. Nobody would talk to me, nobody would sit by me—like I had the plague. I don't believe in that superstition stuff. You just do your best. Some of the guys didn't want to say anything, afraid they'd put a jinx on it."

McDougald was one of them. "It was like every other bench when a guy has a no-hitter going," he says. "And Don Larsen was coming in saying he knew he had a no-hitter."

Tension mounted as Larsen retired the dangerous Robinson on a grounder back to the mound to start the eighth. Hodges lined to Carey on a 2-2 pitch for out No. 2 and Amoros flied out to Mantle—24 batters up, 24 retired. When the Yankees went down 1-2-3 in the bottom of the eighth, Maglie completed his day with a five-hit, five-strikeout performance and set the stage for a wild finish.

The crowd gasped and roared with every pitch as Larsen began the fateful ninth against Carl Furillo, who fouled off four pitches before hitting a harmless fly ball to right. Then Dodgers catcher Roy Campanella fouled off one pitch before grounding to second. Only lefthanded pinch hitter Dale Mitchell, a veteran .312 career contact hitter batting for Maglie, stood between Larsen and baseball immortality—and out No. 27 wouldn't be easy.

"He really scared me," said Larsen, who was familiar with the former Cleveland Indians star. "I knew how much pressure he was under. He must have been paralyzed. That made two of us."

Larsen's first pitch was a ball. The second was a called strike. When Mitchell swung at and missed the third, the stadium rocked. A foul ball only delayed the inevitable—a check-swing, called third strike that triggered pandemonium throughout the stadium and a wild Yankee celebration just in front of the mound.

"The umpire called him out on a strike that I thought was outside," McDougald says, recalling Larsen's seventh strikeout. "It was a borderline pitch. I think (Mitchell) was upset, but everybody was on the field so quick he didn't even have a chance to yell at the umpire."

As the Yankee players swarmed around Larsen, Mitchell wheeled around to argue with umpire Babe Pinelli, who was racing off the field after completing work in his last major league game behind the plate. Pinelli later made a special visit to the Yankees' clubhouse to extend his congratulations to the man "with the greatest pinpoint control I have ever seen."

Larsen, admitting "I was a little nervous," remembers watching Pinelli's arm shoot up and feeling an incredible sense of relief. "Then here comes Yogi jumping on me," he says. "My mind sort of went blank. I didn't know it was a perfect game until somebody told me in the clubhouse afterward. I could have walked somebody, there might have been an error—that Dodgers team had a hell of a lineup."

Larsen pitched another three years for the Yankees before bouncing from team to team over the final seven seasons

of a 14-year career. He retired in 1967 with a forgettable career record of 81-91, failing ever again to approach the heights he achieved on that October afternoon in 1956.

"I think about it every day," he says. "Sometimes it's hard to believe it ever happened. I'm glad it did because everybody thinks about that and forgets all the mistakes I made in my career."

Pinelli, who called the perfect game in his final major league contest, poses with Larsen (left) and Berra.

Ask any baseball fan to recall the 1975 World Series—a World Series many would call the greatest in history; a World Series that showcased one of baseball's greatest teams, Cincinnati's Big Red Machine; a World Series that featured some of baseball's greatest players, Joe Morgan ... Carl Yastrzemski ... Pete Rose ... Johnny Bench ... Tony Perez—and the enduring image is of a man they called Pudge.

Carlton Fisk. A then-27-year-old catcher, playing in his fourth full major league season.

Fisk would go on to play 24 years for two major league teams, collecting 2,356 hits and 376 home runs. But he never would come close to matching that 1975 moment in the sun, which came on a cool, damp October night in Boston.

Fisk's Red Sox down in the Series three-games-to-two, score tied at 6, he leads off the bottom of the 12th. There is Fisk, connecting on a "sinker, down and in" from Reds righthander Pat Darcy, launching it high down the line in left field, plenty high to clear the Green Monster. But would it stay right of the foul pole?

There is Fisk, stepping cautiously toward first base, watching his drive, arms held high and waving, imploring, pleading

Game tied, 6-6. Darcy pitching. Fisk takes high and inside, ball one. Freddie Lynn on deck. There have been numerous heroics tonight, both sides. The 0-1 delivery to Fisk. He swings. Long drive, left field! If it stays fair, it's gone! Home run! The Red Sox win! And the Series is tied, three games apiece!
—NED MARTIN, OCTOBER 22, 1975

What a game! This is one of the greatest World Series games of all time!
—CURT GOWDY, OCTOBER 22, 1975

FISK WAVES IT FAIR

The swing (above, left page) decided Game 6 of the 1975 World Series, but the lasting image is Fisk's body-English dance down the first base line, coaxing the ball to stay fair.

4

with the ball. Stay fair. Stay fair. Stay fair.

There is Fisk, arms held high, jubilant now, as the ball clangs off the foul pole. Fair ball. Home run!

"I knew it was gonna go out," Fisk said after the game. "It was just a question of it being fair or foul. The wind must have carried it 15 feet toward the foul pole. I just stood there and watched. I didn't want to miss seeing it go out."

As a 10-second sound bite from the epic we know as baseball history, the moment is profound enough. But when you consider the backdrop for Fisk's defining career moment, it becomes even moreso.

"I tell you this," said Rose. "If the sixth game of this Series didn't turn this country on, there is something wrong. After that show, the Super Bowl had better be up ... up ... up. It's going to have to be spectacular to compete with what we did in that game. I think the Cincinnati Reds are the best team going, but where does that leave the Boston Red Sox?"

This was, after all, the Red Sox who had last won a World Series in 1918, losing two seven-game battles to the Cardinals—in 1946, on Enos Slaughter's Mad Dash, and in 1967, primarily because of the powerful right arm of Bob Gibson.

This was the franchise that had given away the Babe, that had spent the next half century playing in the formidable shadow of the team they sold him to, their American League neighbors, the hated New York Yankees. The franchise that had enjoyed the fruits of such legendary players as Ted Williams, Yaz, Bobby Doerr, Lefty Grove and Jimmie Foxx. Yet, since 1918, it had zero world championships to show for it.

So it was with considerable emotion that the Red Sox returned to storied Fenway Park, down in a World Series three-games-to-two, with their hungry fans and much of America pulling for them to end their 57-year-old drought.

And with them came a little controversy, a holdover from an intense and unforgettable Game 3 at Cincinnati in which the Red Sox had rallied from a 5-1 deficit to tie the game in the ninth, only to lose when they came out on the wrong end of an umpire's decision. In the Reds'

half of the 10th, Cesar Geronimo singled to right and pinch hitter Ed Armbrister, attempting to sacrifice, bunted in front of home plate. Fisk jumped forward to field the bunt, but became tangled with Armbrister. He pushed himself free, fielded the ball and threw wildly, off balance, into center field as Geronimo and Armbrister moved to third and second.

The Red Sox screamed for an interference call, but home plate umpire Larry Barnett disagreed. One out later, Morgan

When Fisk decided Game 6 in the wee hours of a cool Boston morning, he triggered an emotional reaction (left page) that carried over into an exciting Game 7.

4

FISK WAVES IT FAIR

"I was going to make certain I stepped on every little white thing out there, even if I had to straight-arm or kick somebody to do it."

Red Sox catcher Carlton Fisk

Red Sox backup outfielder Carbo delivered in an eighth-inning pinch (above) and then celebrated his sudden star stature (left, right photo) with fellow Game 6 hero Fisk.

singled home Geronimo and the Red Sox had an important victory.

Boston rebounded for a 5-4 victory in Game 4, but a 6-2 Game 5 loss put the Red Sox in a three-games-to-two hole. So when the Series shifted back to Boston, the Red Sox and their fans were on the edge of elimination—and the edge of their seats.

Three days worth of rain only raised the anticipation and level of anxiety. By the time the Series restarted, there weren't many fingernails left in New England. By the time the Game 6 classic ended, there were none.

The Red Sox jumped on top in the first inning, courtesy of a two-out rally that featured singles by Yastrzemski and Fisk and a three-run homer off Reds starter Gary Nolan by center fielder Fred Lynn, who would capture both the MVP and Rookie of the Year honors in his first American League season.

The Reds fought back against Luis Tiant to tie with three runs in the fifth, two scoring on Ken Griffey's triple. Then they took a 6-3 lead, two runs scoring in

the seventh on George Foster's two-out double and another in the eighth on Geronimo's home run.

Trailing by three runs and with six outs remaining—six outs away from another layer of Series heartbreak for a franchise already covered by it—the Red Sox fought back. They tied it in the eighth when unlikely hero Bernie Carbo, who already had hit a pinch-hit home run in the Series, batted for Roger Moret and tied a World Series record with his second pinch homer—a dramatic two-out, three-run shot off Reds reliever Rawly Eastwick.

"I thought all along (Reds manager)

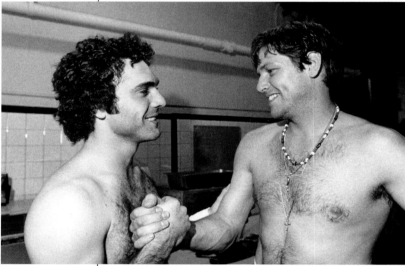

Sparky (Anderson) was going to bring in Will McEnaney and I'd get pulled," Carbo recalled years later in an article that appeared in Baseball Weekly. "I never had any intention of swinging the bat. I knew Sparky would bring him in, I just knew it. Then I hear, 'Batter up!' Batter up? He's going to let me hit?"

Hit he did. "It was a fastball right over the plate, and I was just trying to get a piece of it for a single," Carbo said. "But I knew when I hit it that there was a chance it would go out. Funny thing, but when I got near second base and saw Geronimo standing there looking up, the first thing I thought of was that I had tied a record. Then I realized I'd also tied the score."

The drama was only building. Boston wasted a golden opportunity to win it in the ninth. Second baseman Denny Doyle walked and Yastrzemski singled to right, moving Doyle to third. McEnaney entered the game for Cincinnati and intentionally walked Fisk, loading the bases. With the potential winning run only 90 feet away, Lynn lifted a short, foul fly to left. Doyle shocked everybody in Fenway Park when he took off for the plate. "I hollered, 'No, no!' but apparently he thought I said, 'Go, go!'" Red Sox third base coach Don Zimmer said. "I yelled so much that (Reds third baseman) Pete Rose asked, 'Hey, how many times you gonna scream at him?'" Foster's throw to the plate, several feet off target, still was in plenty of time to nail Doyle for a shocking double play.

When Rico Petrocelli grounded out, the Red Sox had squandered a chance.

The Reds appeared ready to reclaim lost momentum when Rose was hit by a pitch leading off the 11th and Griffey attempted to bunt him along. But Fisk pounced on the ball and fired to second, getting Rose. That was merely an appetizer for the defensive play of the game. With Griffey now stationed on first, Morgan hit a line drive to right that appeared headed for the stands. But right fielder Dwight Evans made a spectacular leaping, one-handed catch, then wheeled around to double up Griffey, who was already on his way to third. "It was gone if I didn't get it," Evans said after the game. "I was playing him deep and when the ball was hit, I didn't think I had a chance, but I had to give it my best shot. I think it was a row or two up in the stands. I turned around to see where I was and just stabbed it."

Anderson called it "the best catch I've seen. ... We'll never see one any better."

The Reds tried their luck again in the 12th with Perez and Foster hitting one-out singles. But both were stranded when Dave Concepcion flied out and Geronimo struck out.

That set the stage for Fisk.

Bench, discussing the decisive 12th in a 1995 interview for the Houston Chron-

icle, said he suspected the end was in sight. "Pat's warming up, and he can barely get it over the plate. I looked over at Sparky and shook my head. He didn't have anything. His arm was sore. There was no chance. It didn't matter if it was Carlton or whoever. We weren't going to get out of that inning. There was going to be enough offense in that inning to beat us."

From his vantage point in the on-deck circle, Fisk was having similar thoughts. "I can remember standing in the on-deck circle before the inning started," Fisk said. "And you just had a feeling something good was going to happen. And I told Freddie (Lynn), 'I'm going to hit one off the wall. Drive me in.'"

At 12:34 a.m., on Darcy's second offering, Fisk turned on the pitch and drove it into baseball lore.

"Darcy was a low-ball pitcher, and Fisk was a low-ball hitter," Griffey told the Houston Chronicle. "Darcy threw it down and in, and when Carlton hit it, I was going, 'Go foul! Go foul!'"

When it didn't, the 35,205 Fenway faithful breathed a sigh of relief, having witnessed not only one of baseball's greatest moments, but one of its all-time greatest games. Never mind that the Reds would rebound to win the World Series the next night with a 4-3 win in Game 7.

"From the inside looking out, it was tough to say how dramatic Game 6 was," Foster told the Chronicle. "Looking at it now, every minute of that game, you could see the intensity. Sometimes in games, you can see a couple of innings when you relax. But the intensity in that game was there in every inning. On every pitch."

Down to the very last one.

4

FISK
WAVES IT
FAIR

Tiant, a two-game winner in the Series, couldn't silence the Reds' bats in Game 6, but Boston's offense came to the rescue.

BASEBALL'S
25 GREATEST
MOMENTS

39

Now here is Henry Aaron. This crowd is up all around. The pitch to him ... bounced it up there, ball one. Henry Aaron in the second inning walked and scored. He's sitting on 714. Here's the pitch by Downing ... swinging ... There's a drive into left-center field. That ball is gonna be ... outa here! It's gone! It's 715! There's a new home run champion of all time! And it's Henry Aaron!

—MILO HAMILTON, APRIL 8, 1974

5

HAMMERIN' HANK AND THE BABE

It was a soaring drive that barely cleared the 385-foot sign in left-center field, a typical home run in the life of Hank Aaron. It was modest and unpretentious, not unlike the man it would represent in the record book for a baseball eternity. As the ball cut through the wet, chilly air on a festive night in Atlanta, the sports world prepared to coronate a new king and demote a legend.

"Now I can consider myself one of the best," Aaron proclaimed in the most regal tones he could muster after hitting career home run No. 715 and supplanting the all-time record of former New York Yankees

great Babe Ruth. "Maybe not the best because a lot of great ones have played this game—Joe DiMaggio, Willie Mays, Jackie Robinson. ... But I think I can fit in there somewhere."

"Somewhere" in the sometimes larger-than-life scope of baseball history was obviously more than Aaron could comprehend on the historic spring night when he completed a grinding 20-year march by claiming one of the game's most cherished records. His second home run of 1974 came in the season-opener at Atlanta Stadium and was witnessed by 53,775 roaring fans, Georgia Gov. Jimmy Carter, numerous dignitaries and celebrities, a

national television audience and an overflow press corps that included writers and broadcasters from as far away as Japan, South America and Great Britain.

It was obvious before a pitch was thrown that something besides rain was in the air.

"In those days, Atlanta was like the third- or fourth-best team in the West Division," recalls former Dodgers left-hander Al Downing, who drew the starting assignment that night. "It wasn't as if when you went to Atlanta there were like 50,000 people in the stands. If you had 30,000 people, even against the Dodgers, it was considered a good crowd. So you knew it was a unique occasion because they had a

Before and after: Aaron connects for record home run No. 715 (left page) and then enjoys the fruits of his labor (above) with ecstatic teammates.

Aaron, making the most memorable home run trot of his career, picks up an escort between second and third base (top right) before receiving a warm reception at home. Aaron (bottom center) displays the home run ball, which House caught and handed to him (bottom right).

couple of marching bands and an elaborate pregame ceremony."

It was the culmination of a massive buildup to one of the most anticipated moments in sports history. Aaron, at age 40, was coming off an impressive 40-homer 1973 season that had lifted him to 713, one behind Ruth's 39-year-old record. Suddenly he found himself at the center of one of the most intensive media storms ever to hit the airwaves and sports pages around the world. The pressure mounted with every probing question throughout the offseason and intensified during a frenetic spring training.

"The thing I'll always remember is the way he handled himself," recalls former Braves third baseman Darrell Evans, who watched Aaron calmly and cordially tell his story to the press, hour after hour, day after day. "I think that certain people get chosen to handle stuff like that, I really do. Nobody else could have gone through that kind of pressure—nobody. He was amazing."

Former Atlanta reliever Tom House also watched the media circus with a sense of awe.

"We didn't realize he was getting that many death threats," House recalls, referring to Aaron's later revelation of just how deep the pressure really was. "We knew something was up because of the body guards. He really didn't share that much. What I noticed more than anything was the 25 to 30 people who followed him everywhere. This was 1974, a kinder, gentler era. It was strange to see the number of people following him, wanting this or that or whatever.

"The amazing thing about Henry was his ability to put everything aside in a game situation. We never really saw a mood shift, one way or another."

That ability was demonstrated April 4 when Aaron delivered record-tying home run No. 714 with his first swing, on his first at-bat, in the first game of the new season. The three-run shot off Cincinnati right-hander Jack Billingham cleared the left-center field fence at packed Riverfront Stadium and prompted a simple exclamation of pleasure from the man who would be king. "That's a load off my back," Aaron said.

Aaron's presence in the Opening Day lineup had been the subject of some speculation during the week leading up to the season. The Braves had considered benching their right fielder in Cincinnati so he could try to tie and break Ruth's record before home fans in Atlanta. That plan was nixed by commissioner Bowie Kuhn, who told manager Eddie Mathews to play Aaron in at least two of the three Cincinnati games. The edict generated controversy, but the Braves complied and Aaron went 0-for-3 in the series finale after sitting out Game 2.

The Braves treated their packed house to a carnival-like show April 8, complete with a marching band, balloons and fireworks, music from the Atlanta Boys Choir and other theatrics that concluded with Pearl Bailey singing the national anthem. Everybody, including network television officials, were revved up for something that might not happen for weeks.

"There was a sense of purpose about Henry," House says. "You knew it was going to get done that day. The end of the 1973 season; all through spring training. Then on the first pitch of the 1974 season,

he hits one off Billingham to tie the record. There was just kind of a synergy about the whole thing."

The excitement was not limited to the people watching the action, whether at the park or tuned in on national television.

"We were not only players, we were all fans, too," Evans says. "(Aaron) was trying to keep us from having to go through all the media stuff, but I know in my case, I was trying to be part of it. What a great moment to be around. As baseball players or as fans, you really get caught up in all of that. When's it going to happen? When's it going to end? Where am I going to be when it happens? I was hitting in front of him. The ideal situation would be that you're on base when he hits it. What are the odds of that happening?"

Aaron shared the moment with one of his favorite ladies — his mother.

Aaron didn't even take the bat off his shoulder in a second-inning at-bat, walking on Downing's 3-1 pitch. He did score a run, however—the National League-record 2,063rd of his career. His fourth-inning at-bat, with the Braves trailing 3-1 and Evans stationed on first after an error

5

HAMMERIN'
HANK AND
THE BABE

"I'm happy it's over. ...
This is something
I wanted. For years,
I feel I was slighted
by awards and things
like that. I worked hard
to get where I am,
although I never
thought five years ago
I would ever be in
this position."

Braves left fielder Hank Aaron

by shortstop Bill Russell, was a little more memorable.

"When he hit it (on a 1-0 pitch), he hit it in a typical way—you didn't know whether it was going to go," Evans says. "With two out, I had to run hard. I remember getting almost to second base and seeing Buckner climbing the wall and Tom House catch the ball and jump up in the air. Then I thought, 'I have to hurry to get around the bases so I can be the first to shake his hand at home plate.' That was something that all of us had hoped for."

On Aaron's memorable trot around the bases, he received handshakes from three Dodgers infielders and an escort between second and third from two overexuberant young fans. He was greeted at the plate at 9:07 p.m. by ecstatic teammates, who carried him to a spot in front of the dugout where he shared a moment with his 65-year-old father and a long embrace with his emotional mother.

"I had been forewarned that if he hit the home run in the game and I was on the field, there would be a celebration," Downing says. "So when he rounded the bases, crossed home plate, I walked off the mound. I went to the dugout and watched the ceremony. ... To be able to watch him share that with his teammates and his family, that was a great thrill."

A quarter century later, House still relishes his good fortune and the unexpected role he played in baseball history. But it wasn't a simple case of luck. The bullpen crew had planned ahead, with each player manning an assigned area, about 10 yards wide, and agreeing not to infringe on another's territory. The choice bullpen spots closer to the left field line went to those with more seniority, meaning House was positioned toward left-center field.

"If I would have stood perfectly still, the ball would have hit me in the forehead," House says. "It was not a great catch. It all happened like it was slow motion. I remember catching the ball, then running toward home plate as fast as my little legs would carry me. I had to fight my way

through the crowd. When I got to Henry, he was hugging his mother. I remember there was a tear coming down his cheek. That's when the scope of the moment really hit me. It was just incredible emotion. I handed him the ball and he took it and said, 'Thanks kid.' "

The emotion was not lost on Evans, either.

"It was so good to see him let it out," he says. "He was one of the guys. He was a good friend to most of us, a really good teammate. He was a great teacher. He was always open to everybody. We wanted him to finally enjoy it as much as we were. For everybody there, for everybody watching on TV, it was something they'll never forget."

The game was halted for 11 minutes, during which time baseball's new home run king received a special plaque from Braves owner Bill Bartholomay, congratulations from everybody imaginable and a continuous standing ovation from

Record-tying home run No. 714 came on opening day, when Aaron connected off Cincinnati righthander Jack Billingham.

joyous, jumping fans. When the contest resumed, the Braves went on to give starter Ron Reed four fourth-inning runs and an eventual 7-4 victory.

"It's like a blank," Evans says. "I don't even remember the final score."

Through the years, Downing has been asked over and over about the pain he must feel as the victim for one of the most famous home runs in baseball history. It really doesn't hurt at all.

"I've always had the greatest admiration for Henry Aaron," he says. "Maybe guys have some bad experiences, but I look at it like, 'Hey, I got to pitch against Mays, Aaron, McCovey, Kaline.' I'm not going to go around saying it was not a good experience. I've always accepted the challenge of walking out on the mound and pitching against the very best. Some days you win, some days you lose."

And on other days, you do both.

Signs of the great home run chase were everywhere as Aaron worked out before his record-setting game.

BASEBALL'S
25 GREATEST
MOMENTS

45

Gibson ... swings! And a fly ball to deep right field! This is gonna be a home run! Unbelievable! A home run for Gibson! And the Dodgers have won the game, 5-4! I don't believe what I just saw! ... I don't believe what I just saw!

—JACK BUCK, OCTOBER 15, 1988

GIBSON DELIVERS IN A PINCH

The first pitch was a fastball. It had to be a fastball. That was the only pitch to throw to Kirk Gibson that night, at least if Dennis Eckersley was going to keep it in the strike zone. Kirk Gibson, who had no legs, or none that were of much use to him, wasn't going to catch up to a fastball. Especially not a fastball from Eckersley.

And he didn't. His swing was laughable, even though he put a bit of wood to it and

fouled the first pitch high and away into the third base stands. As he did, as he flailed at Eckersley's first pitch, Gibson stumbled out of the batter's box and nearly fell. And Eckersley's resolve was reinforced.

Fastballs. Nothing but fastballs. Fastballs away.

"We even went over it in the meeting before the game," Eckersley says, 11 years later. "You're not supposed to throw him breaking balls. Honestly, I wasn't worried. I

A fist-pumping Gibson (far left) received a warm reception from ecstatic teammates after his game-winning home run in the opener of the World Series.

6

GIBSON DELIVERS IN A PINCH

"When he hit that ball, it was almost surreal. As devastating a blow as it was, I remember running off the field and saying, 'Man, that was unbelievable.'"

A's shortstop Walt Weiss

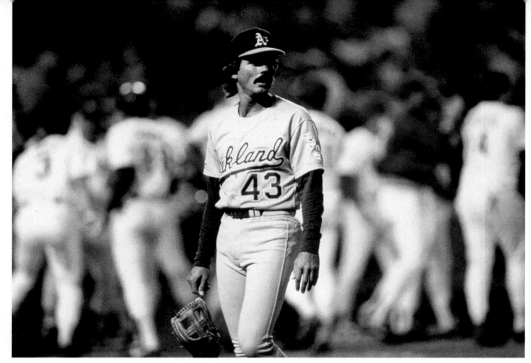

A's closer Eckersley stares in disbelief after surrendering Gibson's Game 1-ending homer as the Dodgers celebrate in the background. Unlikely hero Gibson (right) did a little celebrating of his own after beating the odds.

knew he couldn't get to the fastball."

The second pitch came in, a little lower but still away, another fastball. Gibson's swing was just as ludicrous, just as frail. And once again, he fouled it off into the stands to the left. The strained tendon in his left hamstring and sprained medial collateral ligament in his right knee had robbed his swing of its power base. It was clear that Gibson wouldn't be able to plant and turn on an Eckersley fastball quickly enough or powerfully enough to do any damage.

"I spread out," Gibson said. "I went into my emergency stance. A nice, wide stance. You just don't give in."

The count was 0-and-2. And Oakland, ahead 4-3 with two outs in the bottom of the ninth inning, was one strike away from winning Game 1 in the 1988 World Series. One strike away, with Eckersley on the mound. One strike, and the A's had a man with more saves (45) that year than anyone in the majors, a man who struck out nearly a batter an inning in compiling a 2.35 earned run average, a man who gave up only five home runs that season, trying to get it.

Against Gibson, who 24 hours earlier couldn't so much as jog in his living room, who tried to swing the day before the Series began and couldn't, who was so beat up and certain he couldn't play that

he didn't even arrive at Dodger Stadium in time to be introduced with the rest of the players and coaches in the pre-game ceremonies.

Yet against those overwhelming odds, Gibson hit one of the most extraordinary home runs in World Series history. His two-run shot into the right field pavilion at Dodger Stadium gave the underdog Dodgers a 5-4 victory and propelled them to a stunning 4-1 Series win against an Oakland team that had won a major league-high 104 games, 10 more than Los Angeles.

The story of Gibson's 1988 World Series home run is still, even all these years later, almost too incredible to believe. In the Dodgers' seven-game, down-to-the-wire NLCS win over the Mets during the previous week, he'd looked nearly as feeble as he did in his first few swings against Eckersley. In 26 NLCS at-bats, he hit .154, although he made his four hits count. He managed a 12th-inning home run to win Game 4, and he hit a three-run home run the next day to wrap up Game 5. Too, his sacrifice fly in Game 7 of the NLCS provided the Dodgers with the series-winning RBI.

But in the process, he aggravated his injuries. Twice against the Mets, he dived recklessly into second base, once on a steal and once to break up a double play. By the time the World Series began, he

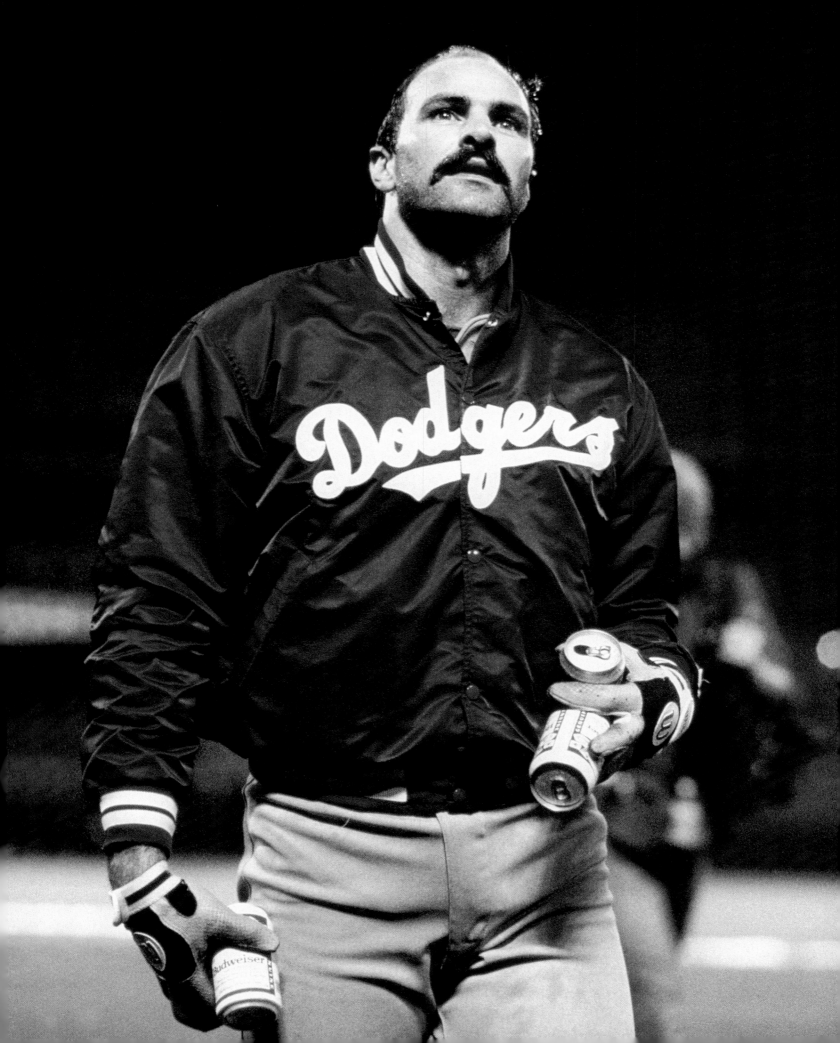

6

GIBSON
DELIVERS
IN A PINCH

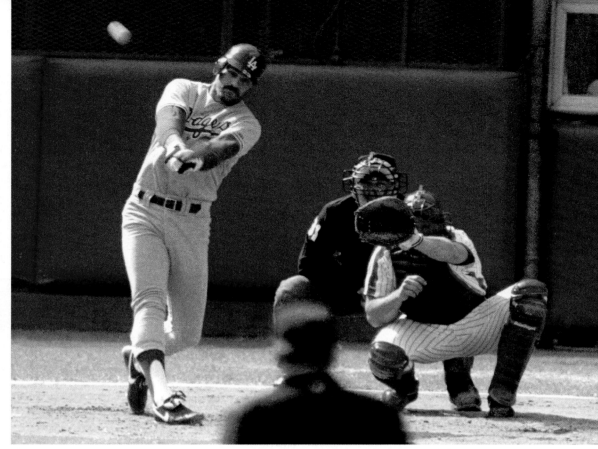

Gibson played with pain during the N.L. Championship Series against New York, but it didn't stop him from hitting a pair of home runs—one a three-run shot in Game 5 (above).

could barely walk. When the Game 1 starting lineups were announced, Gibson hadn't bothered to put his uniform on. Dodgers manager Tommy Lasorda started Mickey Hatcher in his spot in left field.

"You take some (cortisone and pain-killer) injections," Gibson said. "You put ice on the knee. You take it off. You put ice on again. You take it off. The introductions start. You know, it's depressing and demoralizing that you can't be out there. That's what you live for, to play in those situations . . . So all through the game, while I'm icing, I'm working on it. Then, here's the bottom of the eighth, then the top of the ninth. I'm sitting there in the trainer's room in my shorts, and something in my head says, 'It's time to get dressed.' So I tell Mitch Poole (a bat-boy) to get the batting tee set up so I can start hitting some balls. I hit about 15 or 20 balls and said, 'Go get Tommy'."

Lasorda's version:

"Every inning, I would go into the training room. I'd stand in the doorway and say, 'Hey, big boy, how do you feel?' And he'd turn both thumbs down. So I'd go back out. Every inning. Meanwhile,

(broadcaster) Vin Scully is telling everybody in the world that he's in there packed with ice and there's no way he can play.

"Just before we went to bat in the bottom of the ninth, the kid (Poole) comes up to me and says, 'Hey, Gibson wants to see you up in the runway.' So I run up there and he's got his spikes on. He's got his shoes, his socks and his pants; everything but his outer shirt. I say, 'What is it, big boy?' He says, 'I think I can hit for you.' Boom, I turned right around and got out of there before he changed his mind."

As the ninth inning unfolded, Lasorda had Gibson stay out of sight in the runway, so the A's wouldn't know he was available. Eckersley easily retired Mike Scioscia and Jeff Hamilton, the first two hitters. Lasorda sent Mike Davis up to pinch-hit for Alfredo Griffin, and put weak-hitting Dave Anderson (.249, with only two home runs in '88) in the on-deck circle as a decoy pinch-hitter for the pitcher, Alejandro Pena. Eckersley bit on the decoy, pitching too carefully to Davis. He walked him.

Then, as the crowd erupted, Gibson limped out of the dugout. And promptly took his flimsy, helpless swings at Eckersley's first two fastballs. The A's were one strike away.

It took Gibson another six, painful pitches to do it, to connect. On Eckersley's third delivery, another fastball, he dribbled a foul ball down the first-base line and limped a few feeble steps after it in case it trickled fair. It didn't. Eckersley wasted his fourth pitch, a fastball outside. The fifth pitch was another fastball, and Gibson fouled it off to the left again. The sixth was high and outside, Eckersley sticking to the game plan: Nothin' but fastballs.

On the seventh pitch, a ball, Davis stole second. Now another option opened up for the A's. With first base open, they could walk Gibson and pitch to leadoff hitter Steve Sax. But Eckersley already had two strikes, a full count, on a hitter who could barely swing. He went with the percentages. He pitched to him.

But his eighth pitch, curiously, deviated from the blueprint. Oakland catcher Ron Hassey signaled for a slider, and Eckersley threw it. Now, depending on which book of baseball logic you read, a breaking ball at that point in the at-bat is either sensible or insane. On another night, maybe Eckersley had Gibson perfectly set up for a slider. But on this night, the slider was the only pitch in Eckersley's repertoire that Gibson, hobbled and all-but-hopeless, could hit out of the park.

"I got the count to 3-and-2," Gibson says. "So I stepped out of the box and remembered what our scouting report said. It said that at 3-and-2, Eckersley throws a backdoor slider. And the first thing Mel Didier (the scout) had told me going into the Series was, 'Partner, as sure as I'm standing here breathing, he's going to throw you a backdoor slider if he gets you to 3-and-2.'

"So when I called time and stepped out of the box, I looked at Eckersley and I said to myself, 'Partner, as sure as I'm standing here breathing, you're going to throw me that 3-and-2 backdoor slider.' And I got it. He threw it. And I did it."

The home-run swing was not a thing of beauty. Gibson still looked off-balance, and he still got very little drive from his legs. But he turned into the pitch, and somehow found the power in his wrists to send Dodger Stadium into pandemonium.

Four steps down the first-base line, Gibson saw the ball clear the right-field fence, over the head of Jose Canseco, and he pumped his fist over his head. As he neared second base—it seemed to take him forever to get there—he threw two exultant body shots into the air in front of him. By the time he doddered toward home, the rest of the Dodgers were crowded around the plate, waiting to mob him.

"The first thing I was thinking about," Gibson says, "was that I came through for my team. Secondly, I was thinking about all the things that had been said about me through my career. Some of them were nice, and some of them were not so nice. Maybe some of them were deserved and some of them weren't deserved. But when things are said about you, when people talk about you, it hurts the people you care about, like your parents or your good friends or your loyal fans. I always used to tell my parents and my good friends and my loyal fans, 'Just suck it up. Keep your mouth shut. Our day will come.'

"So when I was running the bases, I thought, 'It's our day.' "

6

GIBSON
DELIVERS
IN A PINCH

Gibson's homer sparked the Dodgers' five-game Series win over the favored A's and a celebration by Lasorda (right) and team vice president Fred Claire.

Swing and a shot into the corner. It might make it! There it is: 62, folks! It just got over the left field wall in the corner, and we have a new home run champion! A new Sultan of Swat! It's Mark McGwire! He touches them all. Unbelievable.

—MIKE SHANNON, SEPTEMBER 8, 1998

7

62 AND BEYOND

MARK McGWIRE 1B AVG .296 | 46 CHI 43 STL 4 2 0 AND 0 OUT 2 | NEWS NINE | 22 DET 59 CWS | 0 5 38 MIL 4 7 72 PIT | 7 8 F | Hard

Pitchers and catchers do this before every game. They analyze the hitters they're about to face. They talk about how to get them out. They put together a game plan. And so late in the afternoon of September 8, 1998, Scott Servais and Steve Trachsel did what they always did. They huddled in the visiting clubhouse at Busch Stadium and talked about the Cardinals.

Except there was really only one Cardinal to talk about. There was really only Mark McGwire.

"Look, he's going to break the record," Trachsel, the starting pitcher for the Cubs

that fateful day, told his catcher. "I know that. But you know what? He ain't going to break it off me."

"Great," said Servais. "That's fine. If we can get him out a couple of times and walk him a couple of times, that's fine. Let's don't pitch to him if we don't have to."

And in McGwire's first at-bat, in the first inning, they didn't have to. Two men were out; nobody was on base. There was little danger in walking him in that situation. So Trachsel, who took a 14-7 record and a 4.20 earned run average into the game, threw three straight balls—one outside, one inside, and the third low and then tried to sneak a strike

McGwire lit up Busch Stadium when he drove his 62nd home run over the left field fence in a historic 1998 at-bat.

onto the inside corner of the plate. McGwire swung and grounded out to the Cubs' shortstop, Jose Hernandez.

The record would have to wait. The 43,688 fans crammed into Busch Stadium would have to wait. The millions and millions of television viewers tuned in around the nation and the world would have to wait. Home run No. 62, the one that would push Roger Maris into second place and Babe Ruth into third, the one that would break the most revered record in baseball, would have to wait.

But only for a very short while.

When McGwire stepped to the plate to face Trachsel in the fourth inning with one out and the bases empty again, he didn't give the Cubs a chance to pitch around him. Trachsel tried to come low and inside with his first pitch, but his aim wasn't true. The ball strayed out and over the plate, directly into McGwire's happy zone.

62 AND BEYOND

"It's just a home run. We lost the ballgame. That's what is the most disappointing."

Cubs starting pitcher Steve Trachsel

"It was about shin high," Trachsel said. "It was off the inside part of the plate. I've gotten him out with that pitch before."

But not this time. It was 8:18 p.m., Central Daylight Time, a Tuesday night. And the darkness that had thought to descend in St. Louis was bounced back up toward the disappearing sun by the light of thousands of flash bulbs popping, seemingly, out of every other Busch Stadium seat as McGwire unleashed the most devastating swing the game has known. He hit a line drive, a low sinking hook of a line drive to left field that disappeared over the fence so quickly that McGwire was barely out of the batter's box when he officially became the single-season Home Run King.

The game was the 145th of the Car-dinals' season. It took Maris 161 games to hit his 61.

"I tell you what," McGwire said in the hours just after he hit his 62nd. "For the last week and a half, my stomach has been turning. My heart has been beating a million miles a minute. To do it this fast... I don't know. I just give thanks to the Man upstairs, and all of them—Roger Maris, Babe Ruth —everybody who is watching up there. What a feat."

Indeed. The feat was all but unthink-able.

Maris's dusty, 37-year-old mark had been set so far in the past that it had be-come an inalienable American certainty for generations of baseball fans, an un-breakable record. But McGwire, who had hit 58 and 52 home runs in the two pre-vious seasons, served notice with a grand slam on Opening Day of 1998 that his challenge that year was to be taken seriously. He had 11 by the end of April and 27 by the end of May; and as his home run total grew, so did the excitement of fans around the nation and the world.

It wasn't just the numbers of home runs he hit that caused the stir. It was the dis-tance they traveled, too. Five of McGwire's home runs in '98 sailed longer than 500 feet, including a 545-foot monster to center against the Marlins' Livan Hernandez in May. Another 16 flew farther than 450 feet. And those were just the home runs he hit in games, against pitchers desperate to get him out. His tape-measure performances in pregame batting practice became legendary, "must-see" events themselves for fans everywhere.

Ironically, the 341-foot low line drive that broke Maris' record was the shortest

7

62 AND BEYOND

After McGwire's triumphant trot around the bases (right photo), he got a congratulatory visit from chief home run competitor Sosa (above).

of the 70 home runs he hit in 1998.

By the end of June, McGwire wasn't alone in the chase for the record. The Cubs' Sammy Sosa, a native of the Dominican Republic, hit 20 home runs that month; and for the rest of the summer, those two battled for the major league lead, with both on a pace to better Maris' mark. As the competition heated up, each continually bowed to the other in a feel-good display of mutual respect that lent the rivalry a sense of sportsmanship long absent from the American professional sports scene.

The last stage of McGwire's assault on Ruth and Maris came in a rush. He hit two home runs against Florida September 1, Nos. 56 and 57. He hit another two against the Marlins the very next day, Nos. 58 and 59. Suddenly, he was within one of Ruth's 154-game record of 60 home runs, set in 1927.

"I remember getting on the bus after that second game in Florida," said his teammate and good friend, Cardinals' backup catcher Tom Lampkin. "And he said to me, 'Lamp, I'm going to do it. I'm going to break it.' That was the first time he'd ever acknowledged to me that he was going to do it. He'd said before that he thought he had a real good chance, but he'd never come out and said he was going to do it. That was the first time—that night in Florida."

No. 60, to tie Ruth, came against Cincinnati in Busch Stadium on September 5.

On the morning of September 7, at the beginning of the Cubs-Cardinals series, McGwire and Sosa held a rollicking joint press conference. Sosa had 58 home runs at the time, two behind McGwire.

Which one of you, they were asked, is 'The Man'?

Said Sosa, "He is 'The Man' in the United States. I am 'The Man' in the Dominican Republic."

Said McGwire, "Wouldn't it be great if we just ended up tied? I think it would be beautiful."

That afternoon, McGwire hit No. 61 to tie Maris.

The next day, Trachsel met with Servais in the Cubs' clubhouse and prom-

"I told him to have a little attitude. I told him to be cocky about this thing. I told him he was doing something great. Even three or four weeks ago when the media really started getting into it, he didn't understand. And he was sincere. He actually told me, 'I don't understand what the big deal is.' There was no one else around. It was just him and me. And even in that conversation, he just didn't think it was a big deal. I said, 'Man, I do. I think it's a big deal.'"

Cardinals pitcher Kent Mercker

62 AND BEYOND

ised that McGwire wouldn't set the record with a home run off one of his pitches. By this time, specially-marked balls were being used for every McGwire at-bat to ensure that the record-breaking home run baseball would be retrievable and certifiable.

In the fourth inning, as home plate umpire Steve Rippley handed Servais a ball marked with the identifying number 12, the Cubs' catcher looked at it and said, "Well, here we go. Let's find out if history happens." Rippley smiled and said nothing.

And Trachsel threw the pitch.

"I was set up way inside," Servais said. "I wanted to make sure that if Steve missed with it, he'd miss inside. But he just kind of jerked it right

The Maris boys were on hand for McGwire's record-setting blow, as was the bat their father, Roger, used to hit No. 61 in 1961.

back over the plate. I remember reaching for the ball across my body. I was reaching across. And the ball never got there."

For the first time in 123 seasons, someone started a 62nd home run trot.

"I'd been trying to imagine what it was going to feel like, doing that," McGwire said. "I was sort of telling myself, 'I think I'll be floating.' And I sure in heck was floating. I just remember briefly shaking some of the players' hands and, you know, signaling to the dugout and to the Cubs. And then, after that, I just hope I didn't

act foolish."

He nearly did. He nearly did the most foolish thing a player can do. He nearly didn't step on first base. As he approached it, he raised both fists over his head in triumph and jumped into the arms of the Cardinals' first base coach Dave McKay—and missed the bag. McKay had to push him back to touch it before McGwire could continue on to second.

The next 11 minutes—which is how long it took for players, fans, and baseball itself to regain the composure to continue the game—were simply magnificent. On the other side of first, McGwire was hugged by Chicago first baseman Mark Grace. Before he reached second, the Cubs' Mickey Morandini shook his hand. Between second and third, the shortstop, Hernandez, did the same. As McGwire neared third, Gary Gaetti, who'd started the season with the Cardinals, embraced him. On the last leg of the circuit, he turned toward the third base stands and saluted the fans and his family. And in front of home, Servais stopped him six feet from the plate for another bearhug from the enemy.

Then came a mob scene of teammates who scrummed around him as if they'd just won the World Series. McGwire found his son, Matt, the Cardinals' bat boy, and lifted him into the air. At that point, McGwire did a strange and wonderful thing. He trotted to the box seats at the end of the Cardinals' dugout and climbed over the wall to reach the Maris family. There were hugs, meaningful hugs, all around for the four sons and the daughter of the man whose record McGwire had just broken, the man whose own record-breaking 61st home run trot in 1961 at Yankee Stadium had been completed without a single acknowledgement from the opposing Red Sox infielders.

But the best was yet to come. Some-

McGwire was both resourceful and explosive in his season of triumph.

"I am almost speechless. I mean, I have been talking about this since January, and I get to 61. It is one swing away, and then the next thing you know, I hit a ball that all of a sudden disappeared on me. I tell you what: I totally believe in fate, and I believe that is what happened this week. I thank the Man upstairs."

Mark McGwire

how, the Cubs' Sosa sneaked in from right field. McGwire and Sosa, who finished the season with 66 home runs, embraced once, then twice. Then they shared their own private post-home run rituals, Sosa playfully punching McGwire in the stomach and McGwire playfully punching back; and McGwire blowing Sosa's favorite two-fingered kiss, the one the Cubs' right fielder blew in honor of his mother after every home run.

It was the pinnacle for a home run race that was the happiest, most passionate and most competitive in the history of the game.

7

62 AND BEYOND

So the winning run is at second base with two out. Three and two to Mookie Wilson. ... A little roller up along first ... behind the bag ... it gets through Buckner! Here comes Knight! And the Mets win it!

—VIN SCULLY, OCTOBER 26, 1986

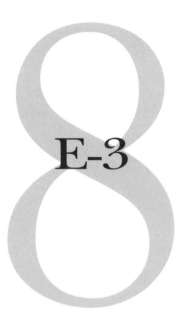

8

E-3

The mere mention of his name creates shockwaves. He's scorned in Boston, ridiculed in New York and pitied by the rest of the baseball world. It's a gross injustice. Bill Buckner, the ultimate gamer, collected 2,715 hits, batted .289 and won a National League batting championship over a 22-year baseball career that most players would die for, but the three-time 100-RBI man will never escape the infamy of an October night in 1986 when he let an innocent-looking ground ball scoot between his legs.

"You have to look at the whole game," says former Red Sox righthander Bob Stanley, who threw the 10th-inning pitch that New York Mets left fielder Mookie Wilson slapped toward Buckner with two

Boston catcher Gedman (right) dejectedly watches Knight step on the plate with the winning run, much to the delight of his ecstatic Mets teammates.

8

E-3

The umpire signals fair as the ball bounces past Buckner and into baseball infamy.

"I think that's the press. The players don't have to have a goat. We just look at a lot of times in a ballgame where we should have done something a little better. Not the one instance that everybody talks about. A lot of things happened before Bill Buckner missed the ground ball."

Red Sox center fielder Dave Henderson

out and the game tied in World Series Game 6. "We left 14 men on base. That game is always remembered for the last thing that happened and that's a shame for Buckner because he was such a great player."

To appreciate the magnitude of Buckner's game-ending error, it's necessary to think back to 1918—the last time a Red Sox team won a World Series. The 68-year drought had become a part of Boston folklore—the Curse of the Bambino—traced to the ill-advised January 1920 sale of promising lefthanded pitcher and World Series hero Babe Ruth to the New York Yankees. Superstitious or not, the legend had played out through three seven-game Series losses over almost seven decades of frustration.

"You're talking to a guy from California who didn't know much about Boston history," recalls former Red Sox center fielder Dave Henderson. "Just that they'd lost a few. And I wasn't really caught up in that

jinx thing everybody was talking about."

Henderson's disdain would be severely tested. The Red Sox appeared primed to end that jinx when they took a three-games-to-two lead into Game 6 of the 1986 World Series at New York's Shea Stadium and concluded the regulation nine innings locked in a 3-3 tie. What would transpire in an incredible 10th inning could have been written and produced by Rod Serling, scripted and directed by Alfred Hitchcock. It was a classic, complete with the granddaddy of surprise endings.

The storyline started, fittingly, with Henderson—the man most responsible for getting the East Division-champion Red Sox past California in the American League Championship Series. Playing as a defensive replacement in the ALCS, Henderson had brought the Red Sox back from the dead in Game 5 with a pennant-saving two-out, two-run, ninth-inning home run and a game-winning sacrifice fly in the 11th. Playing as a regular in the

World Series, he led off the 10th inning of Game 6 with a home run off Mets reliever Rick Aguilera.

"This is a totally different scenario for me," Henderson says. "I'm playing on a bad knee, putting off surgery, I'm converted from a defensive replacement to a player now because I'm hot—I'm hitting .400, hitting home runs in the World Series, now I'm a player to be reckoned with. I pat myself on the back a lot more for hitting the home run in Game 6 than the home run in (ALCS) Game 5. There's no comparison. The Game 5 home run is just a guy with power who happens to hit a home run. But Game 6 vs. the Mets, I'm a guy with power the other team knows not to mess with because he can still get the job done."

Suddenly, the "jinxed" Red Sox were three outs away from a championship. And a Wade Boggs double and Marty Barrett single increased Boston's lead to 5-3. The city of Boston was primed for a knock-down, drag-out celebration when Mets Wally Backman and Keith Hernandez were retired on fly balls to open the bottom of the 10th by Boston reliever Calvin Schiraldi. New York City was preparing for a funeral.

"I was supposed to start (the 10th) inning," Stanley recalls. "When we were tied, I was warming up and the phone rang and they said I was the pitcher in the next inning. Then

E-3

Henderson hit the home run and the phone rang and they said Schiraldi was going back out there. Who knows what would have happened? I could come into the game tied, but I couldn't come in with a two-run lead."

Manager John McNamara's decision to stick with Schiraldi, who had surrendered a game-tying eighth-inning run after

While the Mets had reason to celebrate their great Series comeback, Red Sox first baseman Buckner was left to contemplate the error of his ways.

relieving starter Roger Clemens, looked good until Mets catcher Gary Carter singled on a 2-1 pitch and rookie Kevin Mitchell, batting for Aguilera, singled on a one-strike pitch, putting the tying runs on first and second. Suddenly-hopeful Mets fans came to life as third baseman Ray Knight stepped to the plate, hoping to atone for a fifth-inning throwing error that had resulted in a Boston run.

"When I came into the dugout in the bottom of the 10th, I grabbed a bat from the rack and hoped I'd get a chance to hit," Knight told reporters after the game. "I hoped that I'd get a chance to redeem myself for the error. I didn't want to be the goat who lost the last game of the World Series."

Knight looked overmatched when Schiraldi jumped ahead 0-2, putting the Red Sox within one strike of their elusive championship. But he made contact with the next pitch and looped a single into center field, driving home Carter and sending Mitchell to third. With the score now 5-4 and the tying run only 90 feet away at third base, McNamara made the call for Stanley. He would battle the switch-hitting Wilson in one of the epic at-bats in baseball history.

Wilson fouled off Stanley's first pitch and took two balls. Another foul brought the Red Sox to within a strike of the championship for a second time and two more fouls thickened the tension.

"It was just Mookie Wilson, a slap hitter, trying to put the ball into play and use his speed," says Henderson. "It was cut and dried. Our scouting reports told us Mookie wasn't going to hit the ball too far, a little line drive or a ground ball. Stanley was a sinker-ball pitcher so he probably was going to hit a grounder."

For Stanley, who already had thrown

six pitches, it was a matter of keeping his concentration and not giving in to the hitter. "You gotta just keep going at him," he says. "I was always taught to compete with my best pitch, my sinker."

Pitch No. 7 gave the game a whole new perspective. "From center field, I had the best vantage point in the ballpark," Henderson says. "The pitch is a fast sinker away by Stanley, at least it's supposed to be. Rich Gedman sets up away and he throws the ball and it almost hits Mookie."

The wild pitch whizzed past Gedman and Mitchell raced home with the tying run. Knight, the potential winning run, trotted to second.

"I hesitated," Mitchell said after the game. "I couldn't see it. Gedman blocked my view. Then I saw the ball get by him and I ran. I didn't think nothing like that would happen."

But that was merely the appetizer. With the count now 3-and-2, Wilson fouled off Stanley's eighth pitch ... and his ninth.

> "I always say we lost the World Series like we won the American League championship."
>
> **Red Sox pitcher Bob Stanley**

Then he returned to the Mets dugout for a new bat. Pitch No. 10 was a sinker on the outside corner, another strike, and Wilson reached out and slapped a fair-ball grounder—finally—toward Buckner.

"I knew it was going to be a close play at first because the guy runs so well," explained a distraught Buckner, who was playing on two painfully-sore legs. "The ball went skip, skip, skip and didn't come up. The ball missed my glove. I can't remember the last time I missed a ball like that, but I'll remember that one."

Knight raced home from second base with the winning run, leaping and screaming as he crossed the plate and the ball rolled freely down the right field line, no longer the object of anybody's concern. "When I hit third base, I heard (coach) Buddy Harrelson yelling, 'Go, go,' " Knight

said. "I looked over my shoulder and couldn't believe it. When I crossed the plate, I had a tremendous feeling of electricity. I had the shivers." As the Mets mobbed Knight and celebrated their unexpected 6-5 victory, the Red Sox trudged dejectedly off the field, their season extended for one more game. The Mets would win that one, too, and the Bambino's curse would live on in Boston.

The aftermath of one of the most talked-about games in World Series history was wild, the Mets marveling at their near-death experience and the Red Sox lamenting what might have been.

"I'm stunned," said Hernandez, who had returned to the clubhouse after making the second out of the 10th inning, anticipating a Mets loss. "It's a gift."

Aguilera, who was shockingly transformed from goat to winning pitcher, watched the rally from the bench—in stunned disbelief. "You sit there and try to comprehend what we just did," he said. "It's hard to believe. It's something you sit back and say, 'Geez, how did we do it?' "

Manager Davey Johnson had guided the Mets to 108 regular-season victories, but none like this. "Normally, I never run out on the field after a game," he said. "But when I saw where the ball had gone after it went through Buckner, I ran out on the field tonight."

One year after the classic, when emotion had given way to perspective, Knight looked back with a combination of elation and compassion. "I can especially empathize with Buckner," he wrote in THE SPORTING NEWS, "because a couple of innings earlier I had made a very critical error. And I was sure that's the only thing I was going to be remembered for for the rest of my life."

E-3

Shea Stadium fans suspected they were in for a strange Game 6 when a man in a parachute landed near the pitcher's mound in the top of the first inning.

There's a long drive way back in center field ... way back, back! It is ... oh, what a catch by Mays! The runner on second, Doby, is able to go to third. Willie Mays ... just brought this crowd to its feet ... with a catch ... which must have been an optical illusion to a lot of people. Boy!

—JACK BRICKHOUSE, SEPTEMBER 29, 1954

THE CATCH

The ball shot toward the center field bleachers, a guided missile that surely would deliver a World Series victory to the Cleveland Indians—baseball's 1954 superpower. As two runners positioned themselves for a mad sprint home and a dejected pitcher scurried to back up a base, 52,751 gasping New York fans watched impending doom drop like a shroud over their underdog Giants.

Then it happened. Like some caped crusader racing to deflect a world-threatening bomb at the last possible second, a lone figure converged on baseball history. Willie Mays, the No. 24 on his uniform back providing an enduring image, caught up with his destiny that September afternoon, an act he would repeat many times over a magnificent 22-year Hall of Fame career.

Baseball historians refer to it

reverently as "The Catch." Former teammates and opponents call it the turning point of the Giants' shocking World Series sweep. Mays himself refers to it as something less than extraordinary, a play he never doubted he could make.

"He told me, 'I had it all the way,' " recalls Don Liddle, the Giants' lefthander who threw the pitch that Cleveland slugger Vic Wertz crushed into the outer reaches of New York's Polo Grounds with the score tied 2-2 in the eighth inning of a Game 1 classic. "I've looked at it on TV a thousand times since and my God, what a catch! We did come to expect those kinds of plays from Willie. He was a great ballplayer. They can't convince me there's a better one than Willie Mays. I think he's the greatest ballplayer who ever lived."

He certainly was in the 1954 regular season, when he captured Most Valuable Player honors after batting a National League-leading .345 with 41 home runs and 110 RBIs. Young and infectiously enthusiastic, Mays was just honing the baserunning and defensive abilities that would carry him to lasting fame after missing $2^{1}/_{2}$ seasons to military duty. Everybody knew about Mays, including the American League-champion Indians who would have to deal with him in the Fall Classic. But nobody knew the upper limits of his five-tool talents.

"We had played (the Giants) every spring. They were in Phoenix, we were in Tucson," former Cleveland third baseman Al Rosen recalls. "In those days, we played back and forth. There was no doubt about Willie. He was an electrifying presence on the ballfield. He just brought something special, the way he would play in pepper games, the way he would take ground balls at shortstop, the way he would take batting practice. He had a

9

THE CATCH

verve that was pretty difficult to duplicate."

The Giants, 97-game winners while overcoming Brooklyn for the N.L. pennant, would need all the verve Mays could muster against the powerful Indians, who had won an A.L.-record 111 games to derail the New York Yankees' pennant express. The Indians featured a starting staff with 23-game winners Bob Lemon and Early Wynn, 19-game winner Mike Garcia and aging Bob Feller, who chipped in with a 13-3 record and 3.09 ERA. A.L. batting champ Bobby Avila ignited an offense that centered around first baseman Wertz, center fielder Larry Doby, left fielder Monte Irvin and Rosen.

"That was a great team," says Joe Garagiola, who was ineligible for World Series play after going to the Giants in a late-season deal. "After winning all those games, that Cleveland club had to go into the Series feeling that they were

dominant. And why not? They were good. They weren't overrated."

The Indians struck quickly against Giants starter Sal Maglie in the opener, scoring two first-inning runs on Wertz's triple—his first of four hits. But the Giants fought back against Lemon in the third, scoring one run on a forceout and another on a single by Hank Thompson. That's the way the score remained when Doby walked and Rosen singled to open the eighth, putting runners at first and second with the hot-hitting Wertz stepping to the plate. Giants manager Leo Durocher summoned Liddle out of the bullpen to face the lefthanded hitter, who already had three hits.

"The question was, 'Would he bunt?'" Liddle says. "The first pitch was to find out—a high fastball inside. That's the hardest pitch to bunt and he made no effort. So we go back to pitching to him.

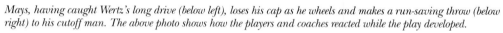

Mays, having caught Wertz's long drive (below left), loses his cap as he wheels and makes a run-saving throw (below right) to his cutoff man. The above photo shows how the players and coaches reacted while the play developed.

He was a low-ball hitter, strictly. The second pitch to him was a fastball up and away for a called strike.

"Then (catcher) Wes (Westrum) trotted out and said, 'Don, he'll bunt.' He came halfway out to the mound. Why they'd switch, I didn't know. But I left that up to Wes. We came high and tight and he bunted foul. Now we've got two strikes and a ball so we show him a curveball away, but it was outside. Then we came back with a fastball up and away and he hit the ball just to the right of dead center field."

Wertz didn't just hit the ball—he crushed it. And only the Polo Grounds, with its spacious center field, could have held the blast that threatened to give the Indians a late-game lead. But Mays, running full speed with head down and

his back to the infield, wasn't about to let that happen.

"I thought we were going to score two runs," Rosen says. "The ball was hit so deep. But when I got to second base I realized if the ball was going to stay in the ballpark, he was going to catch it. And Willie—I don't think there has ever been a better center fielder. He just made a great play and I had to go back to first and it took us out of what potentially might have been the go-ahead runs. That catch may have turned the entire Series."

The ball finally started its descent as it headed for the big green hitter's backdrop to the right field side of the players' clubhouse, about 460 feet from home plate. The streaking Mays interpreted its flight plan, reached toward the wall with glove hand extended over his left shoulder and pulled in the ball. Then,

without the slightest hesitation, he put on the brakes, whirled and fired a strike toward second base as his hat flew off and he tumbled backward onto the field.

"It was an impossible catch, but what amazed me was how quickly he turned and fired it all the way into second base," says Garagiola, who had a bird's-eye view of the play from a window inside the clubhouse. "His throw, which nobody ever talks about, was amazing. I remember he turned quickly and fired the ball right into second base. He had to have skid marks there—that's how quickly he stopped and braced himself to throw."

Doby, the runner at second, tagged and advanced to third. But Rosen, who was nursing a leg injury, retreated to first. Ironically, Liddle didn't see the catch that

"I don't think I ever hit a ball better or harder than that one. Yes, I know I've put balls on the roof of the third deck at Briggs Stadium at Detroit and hit some other real smashes, but this drive, which just ended up as a big out, was tagged as well or better than any of them. I never thought Mays had a chance to get the ball, but he did."

Indians first baseman Vic Wertz

would make him famous.

"I didn't see him catch it," Liddle says. "My duty was to back up a base. With runners on first and second and a ball hit that deep, I didn't know whether to back up home or third base. So I ran over and got between third and home, over by the Cleveland dugout, to see which way the throw might go. When I turned and saw the runners, I knew Willie had caught it."

Liddle was even more amazed after the game when Mays told him a little secret.

"Willie told me later that he had moved in a couple of steps," Liddle says. "I was strictly a low-ball pitcher. I got a lot of ground balls. But Willie didn't know that we had switched, that we weren't going to pitch Wertz low. So he sneaked in a couple of steps, thinking he might be able to throw a runner out at the plate. He had a wonderful arm. And that was a wonderful catch."

Wertz was the only batter Liddle would face. Marv Grissom came on and walked pinch hitter Dale Mitchell to load the bases before striking out pinch hitter Dave Pope and retiring catcher Jim Hegan on a deep fly ball. That, too, was an adventure.

"Hegan hit a ball nearly 400 feet to left with the bases filled and two out in the eighth," said Indians manager Al Lopez after the game. "It looked like a homer, but the wind, blowing toward the right, pulled the ball in so that Monte Irvin was able to make the catch."

Fate wasn't through playing havoc with the Indians, who failed to score in the ninth and 10th. Another ill wind was blowing in the bottom of the 10th when pinch hitter Dusty Rhodes batted for Irvin with two men on base and lofted a pop fly that the wind picked up and carried into the stands, just inside the right field foul pole about 260 feet from home plate. Home run. Giants win!

"The wind blew it out of there," Rhodes recalls. "Bob Lemon threw his glove farther than I hit the ball. Wertz hit a ball 460 feet and I hit one 260, but who cares. We won the game."

In retrospect, Rosen still finds it hard to accept the Giants' 5-2 Game 1 victory and he believes it had a lot to do with what happened afterward—a four-game New York sweep.

"Well, I certainly think it had a great impact," Rosen says. "Obviously, you get the kind of pitching and the potential for scoring enough runs to win, then you see the game leak away with a home run maybe one-half the distance of Wertz's (out). Dusty hit the ball down the right field line. If the ball had been about 2 feet shorter, it could have been caught by our second baseman, Bobby Avila. Obviously, it doesn't make you feel good."

Rhodes, who collected four hits in six at-bats with two homers and seven RBIs in an incredible Series, states it more emphatically.

"I kind of figured they had their hopes up—they had won 111 ballgames that

"(Wertz) hit it pretty good, almost to the wall, which is a ton. But when he hit the ball, I knew if it was in the park Willie was going to catch it. He caught everything else. We thought it was just routine. He had made better catches."

Giants outfielder Dusty Rhodes

year," he says. "But when Willie made that catch in center field, I figure there was a big letdown—especially after we won the first game. Leo had us so fired up we would have beaten anybody after that."

The inspired Giants came back to win the second game, 3-1, and posted 6-2 and 7-4 victories to close out the Indians, many of whom still are stunned almost a half century later. "It was a remarkable year and, unfortunately, it ended in a horrible way," Rosen says. "I have never quite got over it."

Liddle was the Game 4 starter and winner, but his most enduring memories, like most other participants in that Series, occurred in Game 1.

"They hit a ball 460 feet for an out and Dusty hits one 260 feet for a home run," he says. "It don't seem fair, but that's the breaks of baseball. They go against you sometimes, they go for you sometimes. They call it a game of inches and that's really what it is."

Mays took sure victory away from the Indians with his glove, but Rhodes (right) came off the bench to deliver the lethal blow.

Enos Slaughter is on first base with two away. Harry Walker at bat. Bob Klinger on the mound. He takes the stretch. Here's the pitch ... there goes Slaughter. The ball is swung on, there's a line drive going into left-center field. It's in there for a base hit. Culberson fumbles the ball momentarily and Slaughter charges around second, heads for third. Pesky goes into short left field to take the relay from Culberson ... And here comes Enos Slaughter rounding third, he's going to try for home. Here comes the throw and it is not in time. Slaughter scores!

—MEL ALLEN, OCTOBER 15, 1946

THE MAD DASH

10

The play took all of 10 seconds, less time than it takes most people to button a shirt or tie a pair of shoes. It was a flash, a sudden jolt, an unexpected twist to a dramatic plot. Enos Slaughter's Mad Dash was a quick 90-yard sprint from first base to home plate, but the memories and controversy it created will last forever.

"Eno was mad when he got to the ballpark, mad when he played and mad when he left," recalls former St. Louis teammate Joe Garagiola. So it came as no surprise to Cardinals players when Slaughter, a 5-9, 190-pound bundle of energy, thrust himself onto center stage in the eighth

THE MAD DASH

There was plenty to celebrate for (left to right) manager Dyer, Slaughter, George Munger, Kurowski and Garagiola after The Mad Dash.

"The clubhouse was small, not like it is now, and there were people everywhere, screaming and hollering and all the excitement. And then walking out into the clubhouse——that's a feeling, that's what it's all about. ... The bottom line is the little boy in you still wants to be in a World Series."

Cardinals catcher Joe Garagiola

inning of Game 7 of the 1946 World Series—with the gut-wrenching intensity and defiance he brought to baseball every day for 19 Hall of Fame seasons.

From the Cardinals' perspective, Slaughter's daring run decided their third championship in five years. From the perspective of the Boston Red Sox, it tarnished their first World Series appearance since 1918 and branded Johnny Pesky, their outstanding young shortstop, with a "goat" label he never would escape. The moment was typical Slaughter; the reward was lasting fame.

"No, I didn't know it was anything special because I played every game the same way—to win," recalls Slaughter, a six-year veteran who had driven in a National League-leading 130 runs in his first regular season after three years of military service in World War II. "That was just another play as far as I was concerned. I just caught them napping. It was just a heads-up play on my part."

The play developed out of a sense of

urgency. After spotting the Cardinals a 3-1 lead in the Game 7 clincher at St. Louis' Sportsman's Park, the Red Sox had fought back to tie on center fielder Dom DiMaggio's two-out, two-run double in the top of the eighth inning off Harry Brecheen, a two-time Series winner who was working in relief. Momentum clearly was in the Boston dugout.

Slaughter tried to change that when he poked a one-handed single to lead off the bottom of the inning—vintage Slaughter, who was playing with a badly swollen and painful right elbow, courtesy of an errant Joe Dobson fastball in Game 5. But St. Louis hopes sagged when Red Sox reliever Bob Klinger retired Whitey Kurowski and Del Rice as Slaughter remained stuck at first. The Cardinals' right fielder was working the front end of a run-and-hit when Harry Walker lashed a 2-1 pitch into left-center field, touching off the play of the game.

"I was running," says Slaughter, the man known affectionately as Country.

"When the ball went into left-center, I hit second base and I said to myself, 'I can score.' I didn't know whether the ball had been cut off or not. I didn't know nothin'. It was a gutsy play. But, you know, two men out and the winning run, you can't let the grass grow under your feet."

The ball was cut off by center fielder Leon Culberson, who had entered the game when DiMaggio sprained his ankle while rounding first on his earlier double. Culberson bobbled momentarily, then relayed the ball to Pesky in short left field. Pesky's back was to the infield as Slaughter, ignoring third base coach Mike Gonzalez's frantic stop sign, rounded third base and chugged for home.

What happened next has long been a matter of contention. Some observers claim Pesky turned and checked Walker, allowing Slaughter to pick up steam before he made a frantic—and weak—throw home. Others claim Slaughter simply caught him by surprise and his mental lapse cost him the play. Cardinals second baseman Red Schoendienst has another theory.

"It was unfair for (Pesky) because nobody helped him out," Schoendienst says. "His back was to the infield and I know he checked where Eno was at that particular time. When he got the ball, he was still in great position. Eno just kept running."

Boston catcher Roy Partee, who had to move up the third base line to take Pesky's throw as Slaughter slid across the plate, says Pesky was getting help. He just couldn't hear it.

"Culberson came up with the ball and he tossed it practically underhand to Pesky and everybody was yelling for Pesky to

throw it home," Partee recalls. "But he couldn't hear because of the crowd and he started to run in with it. That's when he spotted Slaughter rounding third base. He wound up and threw it sky high instead of low. He tried to reach me on the fly. He should have had him by 20 feet."

Pesky always has seemed a little confused about exactly what happened. But his postgame comments supported the "Slaughter element of surprise" theory.

"When Walker hit the ball, I didn't

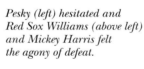

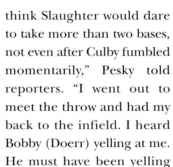

Pesky (left) hesitated and Red Sox Williams (above left) and Mickey Harris felt the agony of defeat.

think Slaughter would dare to take more than two bases, not even after Culby fumbled momentarily," Pesky told reporters. "I went out to meet the throw and had my back to the infield. I heard Bobby (Doerr) yelling at me. He must have been yelling for me to throw home, but I couldn't make out what he was saying because of the noise of the crowd.

"When I turned and saw Slaughter going all the way, I guess I was dumbstruck. He had six or eight steps on me. I just

10

THE MAD DASH

"Everything happened right. It was just one of those things that looked like we were supposed to win. What happened is that Eno just kept running. And I don't think anybody helped Pesky out."

Cardinals second baseman Red Schoendienst

THE MAD DASH

couldn't seem to make myself throw quickly enough and when finally I did get rid of it, I knew I couldn't get him with a .22."

One man who had a bird's-eye view as the play unfolded was Walker, who was credited with an RBI double on what could have been ruled a single and fielder's choice.

"Pesky caught (the relay) right here," Walker said in a 1983 interview, holding his hands in front of his chest. "As Pesky caught the ball, he turned to his right to take a look at me. Then he realized Slaughter was going all the way. Pesky continued his turn—clockwise to his right— and made the throw home. But the throw had nothing on it and was 10 feet wide on the third base side.

"But Pesky didn't do much holding the ball. He simply turned the wrong way. ... Some Red Sox player should have yelled to Pesky that Slaughter was going home. Then Pesky would have paid no attention to me. He would have turned the right way—to his left—and he'd have got Slaughter."

The dash actually took root in Game 1 of the Series, a 3-2 Red Sox victory.

"I tripled in the first game of the Series and on a bad relay throw, (coach) Mike Gonzalez kept me on third base," Slaughter recalls. "So I complained to (manager) Eddie Dyer and he says, 'From now on, if you think you've got a chance to score with two men out you go ahead and gamble and I'll be responsible.' I think I took the Red Sox and (second baseman) Doerr and (third baseman Pinky) Higgins all by surprise."

Garagiola remembers the Game 1 incident.

"He complained to Dyer and Dyer said, 'Whenever you think you can make

it, go.' I was a rookie on the club and I thought to myself, 'Boy, is this the way they do it in the big leagues? You think you can do something and you tell the manager and he just lets you do it and he puts the responsibility on you?' "

Ironically, Garagiola, who pounded out four hits in a 12-3 Game 4 St. Louis victory, didn't see Slaughter's winning dash. He was in the Cardinal trainer's room, courtesy of a Ted Williams foul tip that broke his finger midway through Game 7. But he can imagine how the play unfolded.

"He did a lot of gambling on the element of surprise," Garagiola said. "Eno was an aggressive player. They could have put the Famous Barr building or the Arch in front of him (at third base) and he would have run right up the Arch. Nobody was going to stop him."

The Cardinals had a 4-3 lead, but they weren't out of the woods—not by a long shot. The crowd of 36,143 moved to the

edge of their seats when Rudy York and Doerr singled to open the Boston ninth. But Brecheen, looking for his Series record-tying third victory, got Higgins on a forceout that left runners at first and third, retired Partee on a foul popup and induced pinch-hitter Tom McBride to hit a grounder toward Schoendienst at second. The final out was anything but routine.

"That was the toughest play I ever made in baseball," Schoendienst says. "It didn't look that tough, but I charged it, it took a bad hop and just went up my arm to my left shoulder. I blocked it, smothered it on my chest, reached in with my right hand and flipped to (shortstop Marty) Marion. My heart was beating fast on that play."

The throw forced Higgins and the Cardinals were world champions, capping their comeback from a 3-2 Series deficit. A Fall Classic in which slugging stars Ted Williams (.200) and Stan Musial (.222)

were strangely quiet had been settled by a fiercely competitive gamer who crafted his defining career moment around a daring baserunning maneuver that defied his coach's best judgment.

"Listening to Slaughter and what everybody else said, I don't know what Gonzalez could have said, what he might have said or what he should have said because Slaughter was coming," Garagiola said. "I always put it in the category of when you make it, it's a great play; when you don't make it, it's the dumbest play ever. But that was Slaughter."

Schoendienst remembers his reaction to the play.

"It sure didn't look like he could score," Schoendienst says. "A good throw, they probably would have had him. But the throw was off the plate some, which happens. You can't make a perfect throw every time. It sure looked like he was going to be out from where I was."

A statue depicting Slaughter's dramatic slide across home plate sits outside Busch Stadium, reviving Mad Dash memories and thoughts of downtown victory parades for scores of St. Louis Cardinals fans.

*"I consider myself ... myself ... myself ... the luckiest man ...
luckiest man ... on the face of the earth ... on the face of the earth."*
—LOU GEHRIG, JULY 4, 1939

THE LUCKIEST
MAN ALIVE

11

It has been called the most poignant line from baseball's Gettysburg Address, and the words still echo through time, like they did more than six decades ago through the thick summer air at Yankee Stadium. The speaker was Lou Gehrig, New York's Iron Horse, who was standing before a microphone with head bowed, armed only with a white handkerchief to ward off emotion he couldn't control. Gehrig spoke slowly and evenly to players, former players, baseball executives, dignitaries and the 61,808 tearful fans, who hung on every syllable

11

THE LUCKIEST MAN ALIVE

One of the highlights of Gehrig's special day was an impromptu embrace from former friend and teammate Babe Ruth.

like it might be his last.

July 4, 1939—Lou Gehrig Appreciation Day at The House That Ruth Built. The Babe was there to honor his old teammate, as were many other members of the Yankees' 1927 championship team. New York City Mayor Fiorello La Guardia was on hand; so was Jim Farley, the Postmaster General of the United States. It was a Who's Who outpouring of love and appreciation for a special man.

A dying man.

"Lou Gehrig was a guy who could really hit the ball, was dependable and seemed so durable that many of us thought he could have played forever," recalled outfielder George Selkirk, who

was shocked to discover, along with the rest of his 1939 teammates, that Gehrig's amazing durability was an unfortunate illusion. The sequence of discovery had started on May 2, when the seemingly indestructible first baseman shocked the baseball world by removing himself from the Yankees' lineup after playing a record 2,130 consecutive games.

"I decided last Sunday night (April 30) on this move," Gehrig told stunned reporters. "I haven't been a bit good to the team since the season started. It would not be fair to the boys, to Joe (manager Joe McCarthy) or to the baseball public for me to try going on. In fact, it would not be fair to myself, and I'm the last consideration."

The decision, made before a Tuesday game at Detroit, was delivered to McCarthy behind closed doors. McCarthy later recalled the historic moment.

"I left it up to Lou," he said. "I wanted it to be his decision. The only thing I told him was that I didn't want to see him get hurt. Lou was a great player and a gentleman all the way. All I told him at the time of his decision is that I wanted him to be sure of what he was doing. He told me he was."

Suspicions that something was amiss had been building throughout the early season. The 6-1, 212-pound Gehrig had batted .295 in 1938, his first sub-.300 average in 13 years, and his 29 home runs and 114 RBIs also were uncharacteristically-low numbers. His physical condition had deteriorated over the offseason and his arms were weak and his coordination off when he reported to spring training.

"He was the team captain, our leader," Selkirk said in a 1983 story that appeared in THE SPORTING NEWS. "We all looked to Lou for leadership. We just took him for granted. But by 1939, we knew something was wrong with Lou. But nobody knew what it was."

The decision to leave the lineup was triggered during the April 30 game against Washington, when Gehrig fielded a routine ground ball, flipped to pitcher Johnny Murphy covering first base and then listened to teammates congratulate him for a nice play. "Heavens, has it been that bad?" a proud Gehrig asked himself. It had.

"I was neither surprised nor shocked," outfielder Charlie Keller said in 1983 when asked about Gehrig's decision to sit. "It had to happen. Lou could hardly defend himself anymore. That was my first year on the club. I had heard so much about him. He worked so hard in spring training. Lou was having trouble already at that time. But it just seemed to get worse after that."

Even Yankees opponents noticed something was wrong.

"You could see, like moving around for balls hit to him or near him, that he wasn't like he used to be," recalls former Washington shortstop Cecil Travis. "Nobody knew what it was. You couldn't help but realize that big a change. You could notice it on the field because he wasn't like he was before."

After 14 years of continuous service without missing a game, Gehrig passed the first base baton to Babe Dahlgren on May 2, making his only on-field appearance when he delivered the pregame lineup to the umpires at home plate. The messenger role took everybody by surprise.

"Nobody knew until he went up to home plate to turn in the lineups," outfielder Tommy Henrich recalls. "It was bang, he's not playing. But the way he was playing, you knew something had to happen. McCarthy was asked, 'When are you going to take Lou out of the lineup?' He said, 'I'm not going to take him out; he's going to take himself out.' And that's what happened."

The emotional Yankees pummeled the Tigers, 22-2, with Dahlgren hitting a home run and a double. Gehrig watched the proceedings from the dugout. "We really didn't have anything to celebrate that day, especially with Lou's decison," Selkirk said. Less than a month later, Gehrig traveled to the Mayo Clinic in Rochester, Minn., where he was diagnosed with amyotrophic lateral sclerosis, a neurological disorder for which there was no treatment.

The shocking news spread throughout baseball like wildfire. But the personable,

11

THE LUCKIEST MAN ALIVE

McCarthy gives Gehrig a silver trophy inscribed with the names of his teammates and a poem written in his honor.

11

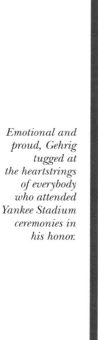

THE LUCKIEST
MAN ALIVE

always-reserved Gehrig, a popular New York icon despite his low-key personality, never lost his cheerful demeanor and he never lost faith that he eventually would return to the field. "Gehrig, I think, was the only guy who didn't think the disease was going to be fatal," Henrich recalls.

Still, there were down moments for the wavy-haired first baseman, who remained with the Yankees throughout the remainder of their championship 1939 season.

"The memory I have more than any other one," said Henrich, "was a sad situation when he came back and he sat down in the middle of the dugout and Lefty Gomez and I are standing on the right-hand side on the top steps, looking at the field. We looked back and Lou was crying. Believe me, he was sobbing.

"And the great Gomez walked past Lou Gehrig and says, 'What the heck, Lou. Now you know how pitchers feel when they get knocked out of the game.' And Gehrig laughed. And I thought, 'Thata boy, Lefty.' That broke the whole thing."

That was but a drop in an emotional bucket that would be filled many times on July 4, when a Yankees-Senators double-header split sandwiched the Gehrig ceremonies. The 40-minute spectacle began with a parade led by the Seventh Regiment Band, which escorted such former stars as Ruth, Bob Meusel, Tony Lazzeri, Mark Koenig, Waite Hoyt, Herb Pennock and Wally Pipp to the center field flagpole for the raising of a banner saluting the 1927 Yankee champions, a team that featured Gehrig as its cleanup hitter.

Emotional and proud, Gehrig tugged at the heartstrings of everybody who attended Yankee Stadium ceremonies in his honor.

BASEBALL'S
25 GREATEST
MOMENTS

"Standing at home plate, I don't imagine that anybody ever made a statement that is better known—about being the luckiest man alive. It was very touching. There were a lot of tears spread out there."

Yankees outfielder Tommy Henrich

The group, dressed in street clothes, was then led to a position, standing shoulder-to-shoulder, near the pitcher's mound. The current Yankees, winners of three straight championships, and the Senators joined the festivities, forming a horseshoe-shaped semicircle around a microphone at home plate. As the crowd began chanting, "We want Lou. We want Lou," Gehrig was led out of the dugout by Yankees president Ed Barrow to a thunderous ovation. He doffed his cap,

Eleanor Gehrig remained a source of love and support well beyond Lou's final moment on the baseball field.

wrung it in his hands and bowed his head, fighting back tears for the first of many times.

"I was lucky to be there," recalls Travis. "It was really emotional, after playing against a fellow like him. It was a sad moment. But it was unbelievable."

After tributes from La Guardia, Farley and Yankees vice president George Ruppert, McCarthy stepped up to the microphone and made an emotional pre-

sentation to the player he had viewed for nine New York seasons as a son. The 2-foot silver trophy, donated by his teammates, was inscribed with the players' names on one side, a sentimental poem penned by writer John Kieran on the other. After stammering through a short speech, McCarthy locked Gehrig in a bear hug, weeping openly on his shoulder.

Other gifts were presented, all of which a shaking Gehrig, his gaze transfixed downward, set on the ground at his feet. When the preliminaries were complete, Gehrig gazed around at his friends and admirers, bowed his head again and fought back the tears as an awkward silence enveloped Yankee Stadium. Master of ceremonies Sid Mercer stepped over to Gehrig, who whispered something in his ear. Mercer stepped back to the microphone and announced, "Ladies and gentlemen, Lou Gehrig has asked me to thank you all for him. He is too moved to speak."

The fans refused his apology, beginning another "We want Lou!" chant. The painfully-modest Gehrig, with a prod from McCarthy, finally obliged, wiping his eyes, blowing his nose and advancing unsteadily to the microphone for what would become known as one of the most gallant and heart-felt speeches ever delivered.

The speech, as penned by Gehrig the night before, was short and sweet:

"Fans, for the past two weeks you have been reading about a bad break I got. Yet today I consider myself the luckiest man on the face of the earth. I have been in ballparks for 17 years, and have never received anything but kindness

11

THE LUCKIEST MAN ALIVE

"It's something
that sort of
lives with you.
You always
remember it."

Washington shortstop
Cecil Travis

and encouragement from you fans. Look at these grand men. Which of you wouldn't consider it the highlight of his career just to associate with them for even one day? Sure I'm lucky. Who wouldn't consider it an honor to have known Jacob Ruppert; also the builder of baseball's greatest empire, Ed Barrow; to have spent six years with that wonderful little fellow, Miller Huggins; then to have spent the next nine years with that outstanding leader, that smart student of psychology—the best manager in baseball today, Joe McCarthy? Who wouldn't feel honored to have roomed with such a grand guy as Bill Dickey? Sure, I'm lucky. When the New York Giants, a team you would give your right arm to beat, and vice versa, sends you a gift—that's something! When everybody down to the groundskeepers and those boys in white coats remember you with trophies—that's something! When you have a wonderful mother-in-law who takes sides with you in squabbles against her own daughter— that's something! When you have a father and mother who work all their lives so that you can have an education and build your body—it's a blessing! When you have a wife who has been a tower of strength, and shown more courage than you dreamed existed—that's the finest I know! So I close in saying that I might have been given a bad break, but I have an awful lot to live for! Thank you."

With the conclusion of the speech, Ruth walked over to this former teammate, threw his arms around Gehrig's neck and embraced him warmly—the first contact between the once-feuding stars since 1934. As cameras snapped the magic moment for posterity, Yankee Stadium almost rocked off its foundation.

"The best scene," Henrich recalled. "After so many years, Ruth and Gehrig got together and it was very meaningful the way Babe—the great Babe—put his arms around Lou. You know that came from the heart. That meant a lot to me because they were on the outs for a couple of years."

When Gehrig returned to the clubhouse, he was near collapse—a

product of the emotional strain. But he recovered quickly, joined the Yankees on the bench for the second game of the doubleheader and then hung around so he could walk out of the stadium with Dickey.

"Bill," he told his friend, "I'm going to remember this day for a long time."

"A long time" was slightly less than two years. When Gehrig died on June 2, 1941, from the disease that forever would be linked to his name, Eleanor, his wife of six years, expressed a sentiment shared by most people Gehrig had touched over his 38-plus years. "I would not have traded two minutes of joy and grief (with Lou) for two decades of anything with any other," she said.

12

REGGIE! REGGIE! REGGIE!

It was as easy as 1-2-3 for Yankees right fielder Jackson, who admired the flight of his third home run (right page) in the decisive sixth game of the World Series against Los Angeles.

It's 10:25 p.m. and it's a cool crisp night at Yankee Stadium. A few blocks away, a building is on fire, but nobody is paying attention because Reggie Jackson is leading off the inning, and the New York Yankees are up, 7-3, on the Los Angeles Dodgers and need just three outs to win their first championship in 15 years.

The 56,407 fans are chanting ... "Reg-gie, Reg-gie, Reg-gie." Going back to the eighth inning of Game 5 of this 1977 World Series, Jackson has hit three home runs on three consecutive swings. He already has tied five players—Hank Bauer, Lou Gehrig, Babe Ruth, Duke Snider and Gene Tenace—by hitting a record-setting four home runs in a World Series.

The crowd's chant grows ... "Reg-gie, Reg-gie, Reg-gie," in part out of reverence for the man Thurman Munson coined Mr. October, in part imploring for yet another blast through the New York air and into Yankee lore.

On the mound for the Dodgers is knuckleballer Charlie Hough, and Jackson is confident that he can do something positive against the righthander. After all, Jackson always had success against knuckleball pitchers, ever since Frank Robinson taught him how to hit the unpredictable pitch while playing winter ball in the Caribbean.

"We were ahead (7-3)," Jackson said in his autobiography. "Tommy Lasorda, the Dodgers manager, had brought Hough, a knuckleballer, in to pitch. I (watched) him warm up, and I wanted to yell over to Lasorda, who I like, and say, 'Tommy, don't you know? ... I love to hit knucklers.'

"I just wanted Charlie Hough to throw me one damn knuckleball. I had nothing to lose. Even if I struck out, I had nothing to lose."

Jackson got his wish and lost only one thing: the ball, as he sent Hough's first pitch soaring into the center field bleachers. With a flip of the bat, and his trademark trot, Yankee Stadium was in bedlam.

Five home runs in the Series; four home runs on four consecutive pitches.

12

REGGIE! REGGIE! REGGIE!

Catcher Munson (15), who didn't see eye-to-eye with Jackson, welcomes him home (below) after his first home run and celebrates (left) with winning pitcher Mike Torrez. Jackson (right page) acknowledges the fans after his third homer.

The Dodger victims of Jackson's three first-pitch Game 6 home runs (left to right): Hooton, Sosa and Hough.

"Reg-gie, Reg-gie, Reg-gie."

Here's Reggie rounding first, as Dodgers first baseman Steve Garvey gives him silent applause by pounding a fist into his glove. Here's manager Billy Martin, the man who feuded over the years with Reggie, greeting him in the dugout with a bearhug.

"It was the happiest moment of my career," Jackson said in his autobiography. "It is the happiest moment of my career. I had been on a ball and chain all year, at least in my mind. I had heard so many negatives about Reggie Jackson. I had been the villain. Couldn't do this. Could do that. And now suddenly I didn't care what the manager or my teammates had said or what the media had written."

"Reg-gie, Reg-gie, Reg-gie."

There were hints before the game that Jackson was going to make history that night. During batting practice, he had hit about 20 balls over the fence, prompting teammate Willie Randolph to suggest that he "save some of those for the game."

Jackson's reply: "There are more where those came from."

As for the Dodgers pitchers, they followed the scouting report to the letter that night, but Jackson made some adjustments.

"The scouting report said that (Jackson) couldn't handle the hard fastball inside," recalls Elias Sosa, who gave up Jackson's second home run of the night. "We couldn't let him extend his arms. The reason he couldn't be stopped was that he was guessing that we were going to pitch him inside. The pitch that I threw to him was an inside fastball and he pulled it very aggressively. Jackson moved a little bit off the plate, and I remember (catcher Steve) Yeager coming to the mound saying we had to stay in on this guy. I threw the fastball right on target. Jackson was looking for that pitch."

Dusty Baker, who was playing left field for the Dodgers, agrees with Sosa. "Jackson was never known for swinging at the first pitch. You've got to give him a lot of credit. A lot of times a hitter doesn't swing at the first pitch. It was obvious that he had a game plan."

The Yankees needed all of Jackson's power that night. With Mike Torrez on the mound, the Dodgers took a 2-0 lead in the first when Garvey tripled into the right field corner, scoring Reggie Smith and Ron Cey. An inning later, the Yankees finally got to Dodgers starter Burt Hooton, who had pitched a complete-game victory in Game 2. Jackson walked on four pitches and Chris Chambliss tied the score with a two-run homer. The next inning, Smith, himself having a Ruthian-type series, put the Dodgers ahead with a solo shot into the right field bleachers.

Then it became's Reggie's show. In the bottom of the fourth, Munson led off with a single. Jackson then hit Hooton's first pitch over the right field wall to give the Yankees a lead they would never relinquish.

"Reg-gie ..."

An inning later, with Randolph on first and the Yankees ahead, 5-3, thanks to Lou Piniella's sacrifice fly, Jackson crushed Sosa's first pitch into the right field seats.

"Reg-gie ..."

And then Jackson rewrote the record book when he hit the third homer off Hough.

12

REGGIE! REGGIE! REGGIE!

Martin and Jackson nearly came to blows (left) in a June game at Boston, but all was forgotten when fans celebrated the Yankees' first title in 15 years.

"Reg-gie ..."

And after the Dodgers had scored a run in the ninth, Torrez, fittingly, ended it by catching Lee Lacy's bunted fly ball.

The Yankees, 15 years since their last world championship, had climbed to the top again.

"Reg-gie, Reg-gie, Reg-gie."

"The momentum just shifted," Dodgers second baseman Davey Lopes said. "You play in New York, and people are going crazy. The likelihood of us tying or going ahead in that game wasn't very good. It's not that we gave up. The adrenaline is pumping and everything is in favor of the Yankees."

The World Series drama that unfolded, of course, was the culmination of a soap opera season for the Yankees. These were the '77 Yankees. The Bronx Zoo. George Steinbrenner. Billy Martin. And Reggie.

It had begun in November of 1976, when Jackson signed a five-year, $2.96 million free-agent contract with the Yankees, a deal that caused resentment among his teammates, especially Munson, who felt he should have been the highest paid player on the team.

To make matters worse, those same teammates declared war on Jackson after a magazine article quoted him as saying, "I'm the straw that stirs the drink. ... Munson thinks he can be the straw that stirs the drink, but he can only stir it bad."

Then came the infamous day—June 18, 1977—at Fenway Park when Jackson and Martin nearly came to blows after Martin pulled Jackson out of the game "for not hustling" on a Jim Rice double. The incident nearly cost Martin his job because he wanted to fight Jackson on national TV after the play.

Martin even refused to put Jackson in the cleanup spot because of his penchant

for strikeouts. It wasn't until early August that Jackson, on Piniella's recommendation, became the fourth-place hitter on a regular basis.

Despite all the controversies, Jackson had one of his best seasons, hitting .286 with 32 home runs and 110 RBIs.

The soap opera continued in the postseason. Before Game 3 of the Series, Munson sarcastically nicknamed Jackson "Mr. October" after Jackson had criticized Martin for using Catfish Hunter, who had pitched poorly in Game 2.

"Reggie's been struggling and would like to be doing better," Munson told writer Steve Jacobson of Newsday. "Billy probably just doesn't realize Reggie is Mr. October."

Going into Game 3, Jackson was hitting .100 in the postseason. But Munson's statement seemed to wake Jackson up. In the next four games, Jackson hit .571, scored a record 10 runs and put on the home run show that would make Ruth proud. For the Series, Jackson hit .450 with a Series-record five home runs and eight RBIs.

"That performance took away everything that was said and done (during the season)," says Torrez, who himself sparkled

"I'm the straw that stirs the drink."
Reggie Jackson

in the Series with two complete-game victories and an ERA of 2.50, "even if it was only for five minutes of our time.

"When we see each other we kid around. I tell him, 'Reggie, you stole my MVP, damn you, because you hit those three measly home runs in a home run porch.' Reggie says, 'Come on, Mike. Give me more credit than that.' "

Jackson took center stage at a Manhattan ticker-tape parade honoring the world-champion Yankees.

BASEBALL'S
25 GREATEST
MOMENTS

91

Ralph Terry gets set. Here's the pitch to Willie. Here's a liner straight to Richardson! The ballgame is over and the World Series is over. ... Willie McCovey hit it like a bullet. A line drive straight to Bobby Richardson. Had that ball got out of his reach, the Giants would have been the winner. Now, it's the Yankees. The final score of the ballgame: The Yankees win it, 1-0.

—LON SIMMONS, OCTOBER 16, 1962

13

MCCOVEY LINES OUT

It was a vicious liner, the kind you might expect off the bat of a 6-4, 225-pound future Hall of Famer. It was about 5 feet off the ground when it whizzed past the pitcher's mound, about 10 feet from home plate before the naked eye could make out its blurred flight path. As the ball streaked menacingly toward right field, 43,948 fans jumped to their feet and a collective gasp sucked the air right out of San Francisco's Candlestick Park.

"When (Willie) McCovey hit the ball, it lifted me right out of my shoes," said New York Yankees veteran Yogi Berra. "I never saw a last game of a World Series more exciting."

McCovey didn't win his two-out, ninth-inning battle against righthander Ralph Terry in the seventh game of the 1962 World Series, but he scared the daylights out of millions of Yankees fans and won everlasting fame—for making an out. The line drive, with San Francisco runners at second and third, was snagged by Bobby Richardson, perfectly positioned at his second base position, to close out a 1-0 Yankees victory and New York's 20th Series championship in 40 years.

"That's a national media thing," says

McCovey launched a World Series-ending missile (left photo), but Yankees second baseman Richardson (right) was in the right place at the right time.

McCovey. "I broke in with a 4-for-4 my rookie year against a Hall of Fame pitcher, Robin Roberts. I hit more grand slams (18) than anybody in National League history. I hit more home runs (521) than any lefthanded hitter in the National League. But that's a national stage when you get into a World Series. Even those people who aren't baseball fans are watching. That out is what many people remember about me."

The moment requires context, starting with the Giants' late-season comeback to catch the Los Angeles Dodgers in an exciting N.L. pennant race and a four-run, ninth-inning rally that secured a 6-4 win over the Dodgers in the decisive third game of a pennant playoff. Beating the powerful Yankees would require another miracle, which seemed to be taking shape when the Giants earned a split in the first six games of a rain-soaked World Series that required 13 days to complete.

Game 7 would be a matchup of righthanded aces—the Giants' Jack Sanford, who had recorded a 2-0 shutout in Game 2, and Terry, who had lost Game 2 before rebounding for a 5-3 victory in Game 5. But Terry came with World Series baggage —he was the victim of Bill Mazeroski's ninth-inning home run that had given Pittsburgh a Game 7 win two years earlier.

"I was thankful to have the opportunity to pitch a seventh game, have a real shot at redemption," recalls Terry, who followed his 1960 disappointment with consecutive 16-3 and 23-12 seasons for the Yankees. "I was thankful to get a second chance because a lot of people in life never get a second chance. And a lot of players never even got into a World Series."

Terry, perhaps inspired by the memory of Mazeroski, was virtually untouchable in Game 7. A single by Sanford ruined his perfect game with two out in the sixth. A McCovey triple in the seventh was wasted by the Giants and Terry, who did not issue a walk, carried a two-hitter into the bottom of the ninth.

But Sanford also was tough, surrendering only one run in the fifth when shortstop Tony Kubek grounded into a double play with the bases loaded. The Yankees loaded the bases with nobody out in the eighth, but lefthander Billy O'Dell

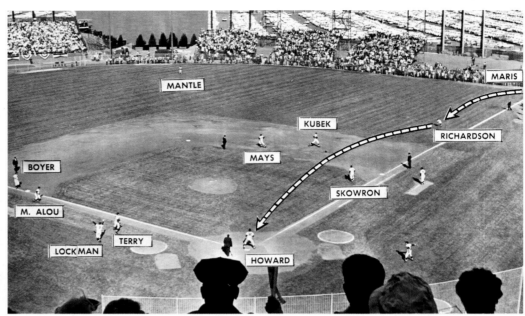

13

MCCOVEY
LINES OUT

This photograph diagrams the key play of San Francisco's ninth-inning rally—the Mays double that came close to tying the game and set the scene for McCovey's World Series-ending line drive.

came to the rescue, retiring the Yankees on a forceout at the plate and another double-play grounder. The stage was set for Terry—either to exorcise a ghost or to replace it with a heart-warming legacy.

"When they started the ninth inning, they sent up Matty Alou to pinch hit (for O'Dell)," Terry recalls. "I'm going to face the 27th hitter and the 28th and 29th— the 9th spot and 1 and 2. Matty laid down the most beautiful drag bunt, I mean what a beautiful bunt. Bobby and I hustled, but we couldn't get it—it was just perfect. Now I know I'm going to have to get into the heart of the order, you know, (Willie) Mays, McCovey and (Orlando) Cepeda."

Felipe Alou, the Giants' leadoff hitter, tried unsuccessfully to bunt and then struck out on a slider in the dirt. Terry also worked over Chuck Hiller, getting him to strike out on a bad pitch. Next up:

Willie Mays, who had hit 49 homers and driven in 141 runs in an outstanding regular season.

"There's only one Willie," says Terry. "I throw him a couple of fastballs inside, trying to make him hit the ball to left and hope he doesn't get the sweet part of the

NBC broadcaster Joe Garagiola interviews winning manager Houk (center, left photo) and loser Dark. Yankees third baseman Clete Boyer (right photo) and other players were frustrated by rain that forced the Series to extend over 13 days.

BASEBALL'S
25 GREATEST
MOMENTS

94

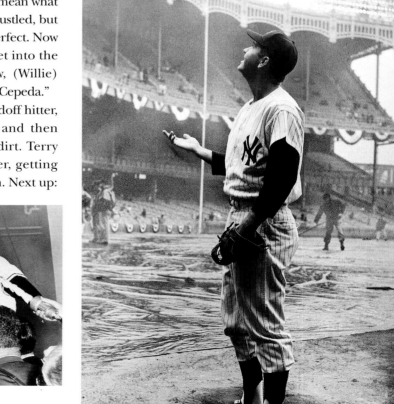

bat on the ball. Then I throw him a fastball, a really good pitch, about knee-high on the outside, right on the black. He was opened up, looking for inside, and he kind of threw his bat at the ball and hit a shot to right field."

Candlestick's soggy outfield grass, combined with the heavy footing on the basepaths, conspired against the Giants. Yankees right fielder Roger Maris raced toward the right field corner, cut off the ball, set and fired a perfect relay to Richardson in short right. Alou, representing the tying run, had to hold at third base as Mays cruised into second.

"When Mays hit the ball down the right field line, Maris made a great play on the ball," Giants manager Al Dark recalls. "If we hadn't had a mid-day rain on that field, we feel like the runner from first base would have scored. But Maris made a great, great play."

"He (Maris) cut it off and made a picture-perfect throw to me," says Richardson. "Now I turned and I don't have a strong arm, but I get rid of the ball quick. My throw is accurate and, as it turned out, it took a big bounce. The third base coach (Whitey Lockman) didn't know it was going to take a big bounce and he held up the runner. I honestly believe he did the right thing."

McCovey watched the play unfold from the on-deck circle. "You would never want a Series to end that way—with a guy thrown out at the plate," he says. "With your fourth and fifth-place hitters coming up, that would be unacceptable."

With the potential tying and winning runs now stationed at third and second, the lefthanded-hitting McCovey stepped to the plate and Yankees manager Ralph Houk walked to the mound. McCovey had three Series hits off Terry—including a home run and a triple—and the fifth-place hitter, the righthanded-hitting Cepeda, was coming off a 114-RBI regular season. Pitch to McCovey or not pitch to McCovey?

"My thought was when Ralph Houk went out there, he would say, 'I want you to throw him one or two pitches; I want

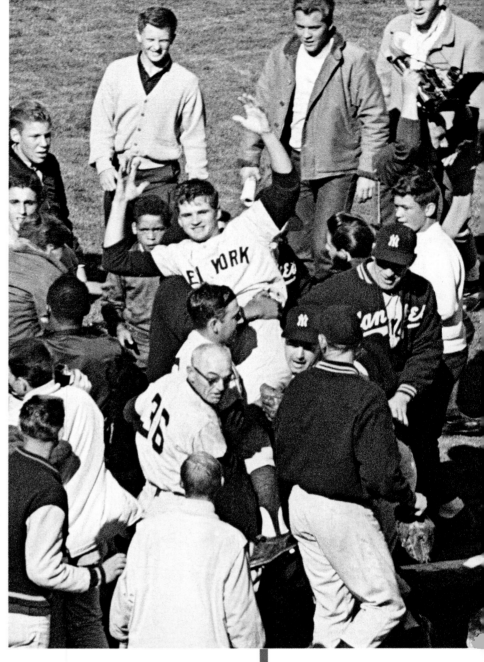

them off the plate,' " Dark recalls. "But when I saw they weren't going to put him on, I thought it was a really big break. McCovey was such a great hitter. And playing in that ballpark, if we got any high fly ball to right field, it was a home run. I felt like we had the best of it."

Terry remembers the conversation like it happened yesterday.

"Houk asked, 'If your control's good, would you rather put McCovey on and pitch to Cepeda?' I said 'No, I'd rather give McCovey good stuff, you know high and tight, low and away, then if we fall behind we can put him on.'

"There wasn't any doubt in my mind. You're on the road, you're in a National League park, you have a National League

Terry, the goat two years earlier when he served up Bill Mazeroski's World Series-ending homer, got a victory ride after shutting out the Giants, a happy reversal of fortune.

BASEBALL'S
25 GREATEST
MOMENTS

95

"He hit a ball sort of like (Mickey) Mantle. Mantle used to hit a ball real hard with overspin. When it left the bat, it really looked like a for-sure base hit. But because of that overspin, it was coming down rapidly. That's why everybody today says it was a great catch. But it really wasn't. The ball came to where I really didn't have to jump."

Yankees second baseman Bobby Richardson

umpire behind the plate in the seventh game, a hostile crowd, and if they squeeze the strike zone on you, you can't worry about a walk. You have to come in and the guy bags one and there goes everything. Plus, Cepeda got three hits the day before."

McCovey was surprised at the decision "considering how I had hit Ralph Terry during the Series." And that surprise might have worked in Terry's favor.

"There was still that element of doubt in my mind that they might pitch around me," McCovey says. "When you're at the plate with that thought in mind, you're not quite as aggressive as when you know they're going to pitch to you. They might try to get me to swing at a bad pitch. All of those elements were working during that at-bat."

Terry came after McCovey, who pulled

thought Richardson was going to be close to it. He took one or two steps to his left and he caught the ball about face high. I was afraid the ball was hit too low to get out of the infield."

McCovey remembers the disappointment as Terry was carried off the field by jubilant teammates.

"It was a fastball and I really wasn't looking fastball," he says. "I still hit it well, but had I been looking fastball, I think that pitch was right in my wheelhouse— that was my home run zone. I think I could possibly have hit that pitch out had I been really looking fastball."

It might be an understatement to say that Richardson was the right man in the right place at the right time. The little second baseman recalls an interesting exchange he had with shortstop Tony

13

MCCOVEY LINES OUT

a long drive foul. The Series-deciding pitch was delivered with the count 1-and-1 and a national audience mesmerized by one of baseball's most dramatic moments.

"I came inside as hard as I could throw it and he hit it and got around on it," Terry says. "He leaned back, got his hands free, but he had to use his wrists to hit it and got a lot of topspin on the ball. As it went by me, it was about 5-foot high. And sure enough, Bobby's right in the hole and it went right at him—he was there waiting for it."

Actually, Richardson took one step to his left, snagged the liner about face high and denied San Francisco its first championship since the Giants moved to the West Coast after the 1957 season.

"He hit a bullet," Dark says, still in agony after more than 36 years. "My instant thought is that it was hit too low. From my vantage point in the dugout, I

Kubek right before the fateful play.

"Ralph Houk came out to talk to Terry and when he did I walked over to second base," he says. "Tony and I roomed together for 10 years and he kids a lot. He says, 'I hope he walks McCovey.' I said, 'Why?' And he says, 'If he hits the ball to you, you've already made two errors in this Series. I'd hate to see you blow one now.' And that's sort of what I was thinking before he hit the ball."

The next day, "Peanuts" comic strip creator Charles Schulz, a Bay Area resident, featured a brooding Charlie Brown wailing, "Why couldn't McCovey have hit the ball just three feet higher?"

At McCovey's Hall of Fame induction years later, reporters asked the former first baseman how he wanted to be remembered. "As the guy who hit the ball six inches over Bobby Richardson's head."

"This was the best-pitched World Series game I've ever seen. And the last out was the biggest out you'll ever see to wind up a 1-0 game."

Former Yankees star
Joe DiMaggio

Deep to left! Yastrzemski will not get it! It's a home run! A three-run homer by Bucky Dent! And the Yankees now lead by a score of 3-2!
—BILL WHITE, OCTOBER 2, 1978

OVER THE GREEN MONSTER

14

By fly ball standards, this was an impressive one—high and deep, a warning-track drifter in most ballparks. But in Boston's sometimes wacky world of Green Monsters and Impossible Dreams, even 5-9, 170-pound shortstops can become heroes. Bucky Dent would have preferred a line drive into the gap, but he settled for a trot into New York Yankees legend.

"Anybody is capable of beating you in that ballpark," says former Yankees closer Goose Gossage, who watched the light-hitting Dent lift a critical home run over the short left field wall at Fenway Park in a one-game playoff to decide the 1978 American League East Division title. "You never take anything for granted in that ballpark because anybody can hit a nice little fly ball into the net like Bucky did. Going into Fenway, you just never know what's going to happen in that ballpark."

Such uncertainty captured the essence of the entire season, a bizarre production in which the Yankees trailed the Red Sox by a whopping 14 games on July 19 and led them by 3½ with two weeks remaining.

When Yankees third baseman Nettles (left, right page) caught a popup for the final out, Gossage (54) jumped into action and led a pennant-clinching celebration made possible by Dent's shocking three-run homer (right).

After the joyful celebration had died down, unlikely home run hitter Dent (right, far right photo) shared locker room honors with Jackson, who made his living as a power hitter.

"I didn't get the fastball exactly where I wanted. I was gonna run it in on (Dent's) hands and I didn't get it in far enough. And then the next pitch I was gonna come with a nasty slider. The ball didn't run in like I wanted it to. I caught too much of the inside corner of the plate."

Red Sox pitcher Mike Torrez

The Yankees bickered through a turbulent first half under deposed manager Billy Martin, then cruised to a 52-21 season-closing run under replacement Bob Lemon. The Red Sox struggled in September, losing 14 of 17 in one ugly stretch, including four straight blowouts to the Yankees in a Fenway Park series dubbed "The Boston Massacre." The Red Sox rebounded to win their final eight games, catching the Yankees on the final day of the season. The hated rivals took 99-63 records into the biggest pressure cooker anybody could imagine.

"We'd played a lot of close, tough games," recalls Yankees first baseman Chris Chambliss. "But to play one game for the whole year ... that was a lot of pressure."

Gossage felt it, too. "As far as the pressure—the World Series pales in comparison," he says. "It's by far the biggest game I ever pitched in. When you play 162 games and it comes down to identical records and you have to play one game for all the marbles, it just doesn't seem fair."

Particularly unfair for the 32,925 Red Sox fans who packed Fenway Park was the prospect of facing Yankees lefthander Ron Guidry, who entered the game with a 24-3 record and sub-2.00 ERA—and a chance to set a modern major league record for winning percentage by a starter. But Guidry would be pitching on three days rest for only the second time all season—and, as always, the Green Monster loomed 310 feet away.

Ironically, Boston's first breakthrough against Guidry came on a second-inning home run by veteran left fielder Carl Yastrzemski—into the right field seats. Red Sox righthander Mike Torrez, a 16-12 performer also working on three days rest, made that run stand up through five innings of a tense pitchers' duel. In the top of the sixth, a Rick Burleson double and Jim Rice single produced a second run and a 2-0 lead, which Torrez carried into the seventh.

"Yeah, I had it going pretty good," recalls Torrez, who had allowed only two hits.

But the Yankees were not ready to concede anything. "I don't think anybody was too ecstatic at that point," Gossage says. "There still was a long way to go."

Torrez retired third baseman Graig Nettles to start the seventh, but Chambliss and Roy White followed with singles. Pinch hitter Jay Spencer, batting for second baseman Brian Doyle, flied out, the injury and then return to the dugout. The delay lasted a little more than a minute, but it seemed a lot longer.

"Yeah, I think it did affect me," Torrez recalls. "I should have thrown a couple of pitches because I was standing on the mound waiting to see what the hell was going on. I should have asked for a delay— just let me throw a couple of pitches, loosen after I've been out there waiting for five minutes.

"I didn't because I was trying to conserve a little energy. Then I say, 'You know what, maybe I should have thrown some.' But I say, 'I'm all right' and I kind of soft-toss a couple to second. I should have asked to throw, but, hey, that's all part of should-have, would-have, but-didn't."

Before Dent returned to the batter's box, another problem had to be resolved.

"I shook that (the foot injury) off, then I looked at my bat and noticed that I had cracked it," Dent recalled in a 1988 story for THE SPORTING NEWS. "Mickey Rivers, who was in the on-deck circle, noticed what had happened and came over to me. He told me I had been using the wrong bat."

The Yankees' batboy brought Dent a fresh bat, which he used to loft Torrez's next pitch over the 37-foot left field wall, giving the Yankees a sudden 3-2 lead.

"When I hit the ball, I knew that I had hit it high enough to hit the wall," he said. "But there were shadows on the net behind the wall and I didn't see the ball land there. I didn't know I had hit a homer until I saw the umpire at first signaling home run with his hand. I couldn't believe it."

Neither could Torrez.

"I was so damn shocked," he said in the locker room after the game. "I thought maybe it was going to be off the wall. Damn, I did not think it was going to go out."

Torrez, shaken up, walked Rivers and was relieved by Bob Stanley. Thurman Munson's double gave the Yankees a 4-2 lead. Reggie Jackson's eighth-inning home

"I had a dream as a kid. I dreamed someday I would hit a home run to win something."

Yankees shortstop Bucky Dent

bringing up Dent. Normally, the Yankee shortstop, who was batting .243 with four home runs entering the playoff, would have been looking over his shoulder for a pinch hitter, too. But regular second baseman Willie Randolph was injured and Fred Stanley, the only other available middle infielder, would have to replace Doyle. If everybody was healthy, "I'd have been gone," Dent admitted.

From such ironies spring some of baseball's most memorable moments.

Dent took Torrez's first pitch low. He took a full cut at the second offering, driving the ball off his left foot for strike one. As Dent hobbled outside the batter's box in obvious pain, Torrez stoically watched the Yankee trainer run to Dent's side, tend to

14

OVER THE GREEN MONSTER

Lemon brought peace and tranquility to the Yankees, who pulled off one of the most amazing comebacks in history and earned their third straight World Series berth.

OVER THE GREEN MONSTER

run lifted the advantage to 5-2, but the game was far from over.

Guidry gave way in the seventh inning to the fireballing Gossage, who was looking for his 27th save. But it wouldn't come easily for the Goose, who was feeling the pressure.

"I didn't pitch particularly well because I was shaking," he recalls. "I was trying to throw the ball through a brick wall. My fastball was straight and, consequently, I wasn't throwing as hard because I was muffling everything."

The Red Sox got to Gossage for four hits and two runs in the bottom of the eighth, cutting the Yankees' lead to 5-4. One run scored on a Yastrzemski single, another on a single by Fred Lynn. The Red Sox resumed their attack in the ninth when Burleson walked and second baseman Jerry Remy lined a ball toward Lou

Yastrzemski drilled a second-inning home run and presented a formidable final obstacle for the Yankees in a tense ninth inning.

Piniella in right field. Piniella took one step, froze and spread his arms to let the world know he had lost the ball in the sun. When it bounced a few feet in front of him, Piniella reacted quickly, extending his gloved hand to his left and stabbing in desperation. Ball landed in glove and Burleson could only advance to second base.

"The ball got into the sun," Gossage says. "It would have been a routine play had

it not got into the sun. He lost it, didn't know where it was, and then makes that spear of the ball. It was a great game-saving catch."

Having averted disaster, Gossage retired Rice on a fly ball to right, with Burleson advancing to third. Everything was on the line as the lefthanded-hitting Yastrzemski stepped into the box.

"It was one of those things where the night before I went to bed and I can see myself tomorrow facing Yaz for the final out," Gossage says. "And here it is: ninth inning, two out and who's up? Yaz. ... My legs were shaking, I was shaking all over, I was just trembling. It was like nothing I had ever faced to that point. I never faced another game like that in my career.

"When Yaz came up, I backed off the mound and I said, 'Well, here it is.' I was holding a great conversation out there with myself and I said, 'What's the worst thing that can happen to you, that I'll be home in Colorado tomorrow elk hunting.' I was putting a life-or-death tag on that thing. ... What happened after that conversation with myself, it was like the weight of the world had been lifted off my shoulders. I just put the game in perspective. ... For the first time in that ballgame, I relaxed."

Gossage threw a ball to Yastrzemski, then fired a fastball that rode in on his hands. He popped it up to third baseman Nettles.

"All I remember about that moment was thinking, 'God, don't let that ball come to me and take a bad hop and hit me in the nose," Dent said. "I didn't care if Yaz hit the ball at me. But I just didn't want it to take any crazy bounces."

Having survived the most pressure-filled game of his career, Gossage retired to the trainer's room to ice his arm. He got a visit from Munson.

"Where did you get that (last) pitch?" the catcher asked. "There was another foot on that fastball."

The Yankees used their 5-4 victory as a springboard to a four-game ALCS win over Kansas City and a six-game World Series win over Los Angeles—New York's second straight championship. But nothing, at least for Gossage, could top that sunny October afternoon at Fenway Park.

"Oh my God, that was beyond description," he says. "You just had to feel this feeling that went through my body. I had never felt it before and I never felt it again. I played in two more World Series (after 1978) and a lot of playoff games. When you played 162 games, you played for six months, and then to come down to one game for all the marbles—it was incredible."

The Yankees dugout applauds a seventh-inning walk to Rivers, who would come around to score New York's fourth run. Rivers was the final batter Boston starter Torrez faced.

It wasn't your average, everyday regular-season home run. The ball jumped off the bat and shot quickly into the short right field seats at Yankee Stadium, where it descended into a sea of fans and touched off a mad scramble. Roger Maris' long, arduous pilgrimage into baseball history was complete and, asterisk or not, the national pastime had a new single-season home run champion.

If the ghost of Babe Ruth objected to the official crowning of a new king, its protestations could not be heard over the roar of 23,154 fans during the final game of the 1961 season. For one day, one unprecedented afternoon in the sports media capital of the world, memories of the loud and lovable Bambino were shrouded by the quiet musings of a proud and private lefthanded slugger from Fargo, N.D.

"Whether I beat Ruth's record or not is for others to say," Maris told reporters after the Yankees' season-closing 1-0 victory over the Boston Red Sox. "But it gives me a wonderful feeling to know that I'm the only man in history to hit 61 home runs. Nobody can take that away from me."

Maris officially beat Ruth's record with a fourth-inning swing that drove a Tracy Stallard fastball into posterity and raised the bar for baseball's most cherished record—the 60-home run season Ruth had fashioned as a member of the 1927 World Series-champion Yankees. But it did not come easy—or without controversy.

"Babe Ruth was a big man in baseball, maybe the biggest ever," Maris said. "I'm not saying I am of his caliber, but I'm glad to say I hit more than he did in a season. I'd like to have done it in 154 games, but since I didn't, I'm glad now that I did it in 162 games."

Much to the chagrin of an unsuspecting Maris, "beating Ruth" had become the consuming focus of his 1961 season, over and above the Yankees' drive for a sixth American League pennant in seven years and the chase for baseball's Holy

Two balls, no strikes on Roger Maris. Here's the windup. Fastball, hit deep to right. This could be it! Way back there! Holy Cow, he did it! Sixty-one for Maris! Look at 'em fight for that ball out there. Holy Cow—what a shot! Another standing ovation for Roger Maris. Sixty-one home runs.
—PHIL RIZZUTO, OCTOBER 1, 1961

THE SUMMER OF 61

Maris' home run swing produced 61 home runs in 1961, one more than the great Babe Ruth (left) managed in 1927.

THE SUMMER OF 61

Homer No. 61 (above) gave Maris a well-deserved sense of relief, which was expressed in the form of a big smile in the postgame media session.

Grail of records. Ruth was the cornerstone of baseball, the name that dominated its record books and the most revered figure in the sport's long and colorful history. Maris, a quiet, no-nonsense interloper on the New York scene, was not just chasing a record—he was trying to destroy a Yankee legend.

And the baseball world, it seemed, was rooting against him.

"I felt like the press was pulling against him, just the opposite of what it was like for (Mark) McGwire (when he assaulted the single-season record in 1998)," former Yankees outfielder Tom Tresh recalls. "I don't think the average fan was pulling for Maris. I think they were pulling for (Mickey) Mantle if anybody was going to beat Ruth's record. It was a very difficult situation, but Roger never backed off."

Yankees broadcaster Phil Rizzuto felt Maris' anguish. "Here was a kid who was so misunderstood," Rizzuto recalls. "Everybody was rooting for Mantle to break the home run record. Poor Maris—he didn't know how to handle the press. They

THE SUMMER
OF 61

The arrow marks the flight pattern of home run No. 61 on the final day of the season in sparsely-populated Yankee Stadium.

Boston's Tracy Stallard

hounded him."

For much of the season, the Yankees' 27-year-old right fielder fought a losing battle against a constant and intense media blitz while competing on the field against Mantle for home run supremacy. It was a vicious circle. The home runs attracted attention; that attention took away the privacy he craved.

"He was basically a very shy guy," recalls Jack Lang, who covered the 1961 Yankees for the Long Island Press. "He did not like all the attention he was getting. But the people who dealt with him regularly found him very accommodating. He sat and answered questions for a long time after games.

"It was heavily covered for that era, but not anywhere near what it would be now. He didn't have anywhere near the pressure that McGwire had. He didn't have TV crews following him around. He had the spotlight on him because he had tied Ruth's record, but he wasn't hounded by TV cameras and the microphones they have nowadays."

But, still, the pressure was enormous.

The chase stirred every emotion, good and bad, for the blunt, always-honest Maris, who brooded over the spotlight he abhorred and wondered why New York fans embraced Mantle as their popular choice to claim Ruth's title. The frustration was doubled by a late-July edict from baseball commissioner Ford Frick that any player who hoped to claim Ruth's record had to do so before his team's 155th game, thus minimizing any achievement that occurred over the final eight games of baseball's new 162-game schedule.

"He hit 61 home runs that season. Ruth hit 60. No, I didn't buy the commissioner's ruling," said former Yankees righthander Bill Stafford.

Throngs of New York fans apparently did, passing up the chance to see Maris go for the record on a beautiful October afternoon. With Mantle knocked out of the chase by a September illness and the Yankees in full control of the A.L.

"I appreciate the fact that he (Stallard) was man enough to pitch to me and to get me out. When he got behind me, he came in with the pitch to try and get me out."

Yankees right fielder Roger Maris

BASEBALL'S 25 GREATEST MOMENTS

107

The Yankees' M&M Boys, Maris (left) and Mantle, shared their thoughts while matching home runs during the historic 1961 season.

"I didn't care too much about what was being said outside the clubhouse. All the players pulled for both of them. They wanted to win ballgames. Mantle pulled for Maris; Maris pulled for Mantle. As long as they're hitting homers, we're scoring runs and winning ballgames. That's all we were interested in."

Yankees pitcher Bill Stafford

standings, Maris had continued his pursuit alone, driving homer No. 59 in the team's 155th game—acceptable under Frick's so-called "asterisk ruling" because the Yankees had played an early-season tie. No. 60 had come in the 159th game, leaving Maris officially short of Ruth's mark. Although Yankee Stadium was only about a third full October 1, the media was there in force to chronicle a memorable piece of baseball history.

"The Babe Ruth ruling affected everything," recalls Boston catcher Russ Nixon, a former Cleveland teammate of Maris who watched the moment unfold from his perch behind home plate. "The Yankees had already clinched the pennant. Every-

body (with the Red Sox) was packed to go home. When the game was over, we really didn't think too much about it. Roger and I had played together and I was happy for him. But the long season was over and we were going home.

"But the New York media—the intensity still was there. They had pounded Mickey and Roger over the last few weeks of the season. Roger still was a small-town guy from Fargo. He liked his privacy. The pounding took a toll on him. I don't remember saying anything to him during the (record-breaking) at-bat, but we talked before the game and he told me he just wanted it to be over. I think he wanted it to be over more than he wanted to hit a home run."

The game developed as a pitching duel between young Boston righthander Stallard and Stafford, who was tuning up for a World Series start. Both pitchers took control early, with Stallard retiring Maris on a fly ball to left fielder Carl Yastrzemski in the first inning. There was one out and nobody on base when Maris returned to the plate in the fourth inning of a scoreless game.

"I knew it was gone the minute I hit it," Maris said. "I can't explain how I felt. I don't know what I was thinking as I rounded the bases. My mind was blank."

"I knew he hit the stuffing out of it," Stallard said, recalling the 2-0 fastball that produced the only run of the game. "But I didn't think it was going to be a home run. I turned around and then saw the thing going way up. I don't feel badly about it at all. Why should I? The guy hit 60 home runs off a bunch of other pitchers in the league before he got me today."

Tresh, who had joined the Yankees as a September callup, recalls the moment with a sense of reverence.

"Just being there, there was electricity and excitement," he says. "Especially over the last couple of weeks. Then he hit No. 60, he tied Babe Ruth and the excitement for me really built. It was almost tense; time was running out.

"It was a great thing for me. I was 22 at the time. The pennant race, the home run race. I was in a locker room with great players sitting around me. I looked around and said, 'Why me? Why do I get to do this?' I was fortunate I had the chance to be with Roger. Roger was a class person. I don't think the public ever really got to know him."

As Maris rounded the bases, Tresh remembers being "really caught up in the excitement. I realized he had broken Babe Ruth's record. A lot of great players had tried and failed. It was just a tremendous feeling."

But unlike future home run milestones that would become nationally televised, choreographed media events, Maris'

Frick's 154-game ruling took some of the luster off Maris' record-setting home run accomplishment.

moment lasted only a few minutes.

"In those days, photographers were allowed on the field and it was like a stampede—trying to take pictures of him crossing the plate, in front of the dugout," Nixon says. "I basically got out of the way. The Yankee players pushed Maris out (to take bows). The whole thing might have lasted about five minutes. That was a long time for those days. But there wasn't a lot of celebration. The game just continued."

Tresh remembers the Yankee players forcing Maris to mug for the crowd.

"Yeah, we pushed him out," he says. "We were having a little fun with him. We had to push him out. He was the type of person who wouldn't have done that on his own. But other than the dugout, I don't think there were any real celebrations."

There was, however, the expected media blitz.

"As fast as we could get into the locker room, the press was swarming everywhere," Tresh says. "It was chaos. Roger's locker was across from mine and there were press people everywhere."

Maris settled in for another long night of questions and pictures, including one with Sal Durante, the 19-year-old Brooklyn truck driver who had caught the historic blow. When the day was over, the strain Maris had felt for so long was obvious, both in his eyes and his words.

"Nobody knows how tired I am," he said. "Naturally, I'm happy I got past that 60 during the season. And (even though) the 61st wasn't hit in 154 games, I'm happy. That's the way it was to be and that's the way it is."

Sal Durante, the young Brooklyn truck driver who was in the right place at the right time, poses with his girlfriend and the 61st home run ball he retrieved.

Now the 2-2. ... Well hit down the left field line. Way back and ... gone! Joe Carter with a three-run homer. The winners and still world champions, the Toronto Blue Jays!

—SEAN MCDONOUGH, OCTOBER 23, 1993

CARTER'S SWING BEATS THE WILD THING

16

Carter found himself at the top of the baseball world after pounding the home run that gave Toronto and Canada a second straight World Series championship.

They were oil and water, opposites who attracted a national spotlight when their destinies clashed on a memorable October night in 1993. One was quiet, workmanlike and amazingly consistent as the leading run producer of the Toronto Blue Jays. The other was eccentric, colorful and aggravatingly unpredictable, the "Wild Thing" of Philadelphia's bullpen. The baseball legacies of Joe Carter and Mitch Williams

forever will be intertwined by one momentous pitch that decided a World Series.

"They haven't made up the word yet to describe what the feeling is. ... Once the ball goes over the fence, it's something you can't believe," said Carter, who electrified a capacity crowd at Toronto's SkyDome with a three-run, ninth-inning home run that gave the Blue Jays a Series-deciding 8-6 win.

"Ain't nobody walking this Earth that feels worse than I do," said Williams, who served up the first come-from-behind Series-ending home run in baseball history. "No excuses. I didn't get the job done."

Oil and water. Success and failure. The thrill of victory, the agony of defeat.

In retrospect, Game 6 provided a refreshing conclusion to a World Series that was more about image than substance—the slick, businesslike Blue Jays, trying to become baseball's first repeat champions since the New York Yankees in 1977 and '78, vs. the disheveled, unrefined, down-and-dirty Phillies, conquerors of the Atlanta Braves (104 regular-season wins) in the N.L. Championship Series. Through five games, fans were not sure whether they were watching a street brawl (Toronto recorded an ugly 15-14 victory in Game 4 to take a three-games-to-one advantage) or a ballet (the Phillies earned a 2-0 life-saving win in Game 5 behind Curt Schilling). What the early Series lacked in grace and style, it more than made up for with unexpected twists and turns.

That pattern would play out—a prospect that appeared unlikely through the first six innings of the finale.

That's because righthander Dave

16

CARTER'S SWING BEATS THE WILD THING

One memorable swing sent Carter into a baserunning euphoria (right) and condemned the Phillies and Williams (right page) to a winter of discontent.

"I was just hoping that something would happen. We just had never quit all year. Same as the Phillies."

Blue Jays manager Cito Gaston

Stewart, backed by an RBI triple and solo home run by designated hitter Paul Molitor, carried a 5-1 lead into the seventh. He had surrendered only two hits—a fourth-inning bloop double by Darren Daulton and run-scoring single by Jim Eisenreich—and the Jays appeared headed for an easy title-clinching win.

"If I'm on my game, then we win the game," Stewart had predicted before taking the mound in Game 6. But the Phillies, displaying the same grit that had carried them to an unexpected World Series appearance, would prove him wrong.

Stewart walked shortstop Kevin Stocker to open the seventh and second baseman Mickey Morandini followed with a single. That brought up center fielder Lenny Dykstra, a little man who had been

carrying a big stick throughout the Series. The feisty Dykstra, nicknamed "Nails" because of his hard-nosed, gritty style of play, already had hit three home runs and earned the everlasting respect of his peers.

"What can you say about Dykstra?" Carter said. "I thought we had the best leadoff hitter in the game (left fielder Rickey Henderson). After not having seen Lenny play over the past three years, I may have to change my mind. Rickey is a great athlete. (But) that little guy can flat-out play."

Dykstra took Stewart to 3-1 and then yanked a fastball into the second deck of the right field stands. SkyDome turned silent as manager Cito Gaston trudged slowly to the mound, the Blue Jays' lead now trimmed to 5-4. Righthander Danny

16

CARTER'S SWING BEATS THE WILD THING

Cox replaced Stewart, but Dykstra had lit a match that wouldn't go out.

"When the red light from the camera goes on, (Dykstra) usually gets the job done," manager Jim Fregosi said. "He thrives on the attention and the excitement you get playing in the postseason."

Mariano Duncan greeted Cox with a single, stole second and scored on a single by third baseman Dave Hollins. After a walk and a single filled the bases, the Phillies scored again on a sacrifice fly by Pete Incaviglia. Toronto's 5-1 lead had quickly transformed into a 6-5 deficit.

Roger Mason, David West and Larry Andersen checked the Blue Jays through the seventh and eighth, lifting the Phillies to within three outs of a seventh game. Nobody doubted the bottom of the ninth would be an adventure when Williams was called from the bullpen in his usual role as stopper.

"Every time (he) pitches, it takes me

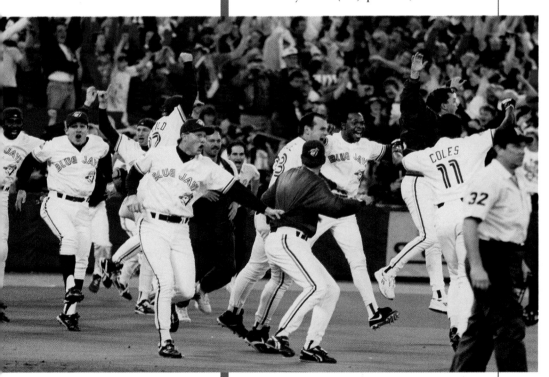

Ecstatic Blue Jays rush the field for the customary championship hugfest.

an extra hour and a vodka martini to get to sleep," Phillies owner Bill Giles had said earlier in the Series. Williams, who had recorded 43 often-frenetic saves during the regular season, had failed badly in Game 4 when he surrendered three runs in two-thirds of an inning as the Blue Jays

rallied for their 15-14 win.

"Mitch has had a lot of critics all year," Dykstra said in defense of his much-criticized teammate. "Yeah, he did make it exciting at times. Everybody knows the story in that. He's got a lot of heart. The bottom line is, he wants the ball and he does his best out there."

Williams started the inning in typical form, walking leadoff hitter Henderson. Williams retired center fielder Devon White on a fly ball, but the hot-hitting Molitor was next. Williams started him off with a strike.

"The first pitch I didn't see," Molitor said later. "The umpire was on the second base side and I lost it in his shirt. I had him move to the other side." Two pitches later, Molitor lined a single to center field, sending Henderson to second. The situation got serious when Carter, who had averaged 31 homers and 112 RBIs over the last eight seasons, stepped to the plate.

"I hadn't faced Mitch since his days in Texas," Carter said. "I didn't get a chance to face him in Philadelphia (during the Series). I knew his velocity wasn't good and the only pitch he was getting over was his slider."

Carter took Williams' first two pitches for balls and his third for a strike. He looked bad on a swinging second strike. "He took something off it and I swung through it," Carter said. "After I got two strikes, I said all I need is a base hit. He threw a slider down and in; he kept it low. When I hit it, I didn't know if it would get out because I lost it in the lights."

Few in the SkyDome crowd or either dugout doubted it would get out. First there was a pause, then a collective gasp before the stadium erupted into a celebration that would last long after Carter had touched home plate. For the first time since 1960 when Pittsburgh's Bill Mazeroski broke a 9-9 tie against the New York Yankees, a World Series ended

Dykstra hit four World Series home runs and did everything he could to get the Phillies to a seventh game, but in the end the Blue Jays had too many weapons at their disposal.

with a home run. For the first time since 1988 and only the second time ever, a World Series game ended on a home run that brought the winning team from behind.

"When he hit it, I couldn't breathe," said Toronto third base coach Nick Leyva. "I knew it was out. When you're down by a run and you're about to get three, you're going to be a world champion—I was pretty good in arithmetic."

Henderson scored the tying run and Molitor, a 37-year-old veteran who batted .500 (12-for-24) while claiming MVP honors, brought home the winner. "I was just about on second base before I knew what had happened," he said. "That next 180 feet—that's about as close as I can get to moonwalking."

Carter didn't have any problem with his dance steps. He tossed his helmet and began a euphoric do-si-do around the bases. He was mobbed and carried off the field by his teammates, did a quick postgame interview and returned to deliver a parade of high fives to fans all around the field. His first stop when he returned to the

clubhouse was the video room.

"I knew what I did," he said, "but I wanted to see how the fans and my teammates reacted. When I saw myself jump up and down, tears came to my eyes. I'm very happy this dream came true."

Carter's euphoria stood in stark contrast to the dejection Williams was suffering in the other clubhouse. He sat at his locker staring straight ahead, hands running through his sweat-soaked hair and eyes bloodshot and tired. "Everybody saw what happened," he said in a monotone voice. "I made a mistake and he hit the mistake. I let my team down today.

"I'm not going to go home and commit suicide or anything. They did what they had to do to win this Series and I let us down in big situations. I have to carry that burden."

Dykstra shared Williams' disappointment, but he refused to assign blame.

"We were so close, but we proved to America and the world that we will not quit," he said. "I really thought it was going seven (games). ... I'm happy I played well and got some hits, but we did not win the World Series, so there's disappointment."

But no second-guessing.

"Mitch has been our closer all year," Fregosi said. "I'm not going to change there. As I told him after the game, he's the one who got us here."

Carter, ironically, had failed to get a hit in his last seven at-bats going into his ninth-inning appearance against Williams. But he wasn't about to miss his date with destiny.

"You always hope it's you in that situation," he said. "This is the biggest day in my career. ... These are the kinds of moments you dream about."

"When I saw that ball go over the wall, it was a dream come true."

Blue Jays DH Paul Molitor

THE NEW IRON MAN

Damion Easley popped up, an easy play; and in short right field, second baseman Manny Alexander squeezed the ball into his glove for the third out in a routine 1-2-3 top of the fifth inning. The California Angels' side was retired.

And a 22-minute, 15-second national love-in began. It started with a buzz from the crowd and grew in crescendo until it seemed to have consumed every lingering drop of the bad blood shed in baseball's dirty little labor war of the two previous seasons, a war that cost the major leagues 669 regular-season games, the 1994 post–season and the passionate goodwill of countless numbers of fans.

The night was September 6, 1995. And the tidal wave of emotion that swept through Baltimore's Camden Yards as the Orioles trotted off the field was so positive and robust, and so timely, that the notion that baseball was saved from itself—and that one man had saved it—was inescapable.

The object of affection, the center of all this attention, was an unassuming, blue-eyed, balding shortstop who had nothing whatsoever to do with the Angels' three outs in the top of the fifth. The object of affection was Cal Ripken Jr., who simply was there. He played. That's all it took. Oh, it didn't hurt that he hit a home run in the Baltimore fourth, a massively-struck line drive high into the left-field seats. But the home run was merely a bonus, a little something extra, an unexpected perk. The bells and whistles from Bangor to Burbank, the groundswell surge of love and euphoria in Baltimore and beyond that sprang forth the moment Easley's

third out made it a bona fide contest, came simply because Ripken played.

For the 2,131st consecutive time.

"The Streak" had finally reached fruition. And the baseball world celebrated it for more than 22 minutes before the game resumed in Camden Yards.

"It's one of those moments in your life that almost seems like a dream," Ripken said. "It doesn't seem like it's happening to you. It seems like you're taken out of your own body and you're actually looking at yourself doing something. It was just a very special night. It was a great celebration for baseball, and it seemed to go perfect in every aspect. It almost seems like a storybook."

It was a national phenomenon. In Boston, some 335 miles up I-95 from Camden Yards, fans stood and applauded for a full five minutes when word reached

17

THE NEW
IRON MAN

*Ripken gave
Baltimore fans
2,131 reasons to
enjoy his streak,
and he spiced his
record-setting day
with a home run.*

Fenway Park that the game in Baltimore had achieved "official" status by progressing through the minimum 4 ½ innings with the Orioles ahead 3-1.

That reaction reverberated through ballparks and beer joints, through living rooms and latitudes across the nation, in every nook and cranny where baseball is celebrated as a visceral link between America's glorious past and the potential in its present and future. Even an American president, Bill Clinton, along with his vice president, Al Gore, stood to cheer and wipe away a tear in the stands.

An unbreakable record, one that had lasted for 56 years, four months and six days, had just been broken. Ripken's presence in the Orioles' lineup that Wednesday night in September pushed Lou Gehrig, the "Iron Horse" who played for the Yankees in 2,130 consecutive games from 1925 to 1939, into second place on the endurance list. The baseball world watched in admiration and reverence as a banner bearing the number "1" unfurled to replace the "0" at the end of "2,130" and mark the moment on the side of the B&O Warehouse beyond the right field stands.

The consecutive-games record would have been worthy of a celebration under any conditions, in any season. But in 1995, baseball was still reeling from the after-effects of the work stoppage and loss of the postseason in 1994. Attendance in ballparks around the major leagues had dropped precipitously, and the game's long-term recovery was anything but certain.

As Ripken neared Gehrig's record, though, fans responded in growing numbers to his work ethic, to his sense of responsibility and devotion to the game. When he broke it, he seemed also to break through the wall of resistance to baseball's re-acceptance in general. The game rather desperately needed a savior. It found the right man for the job in Ripken, a modest, decent spokesman

THE NEW
IRON MAN

"I think, obviously, he was physically and mentally tired. I know all the attention throughout the season was wearing him down mentally and physically. I think he was just relieved it was over, and he just wanted to sit in the dugout for five or 10 minutes and take a break. But his teammates just wouldn't let him do it. All of a sudden, he's going around the park."

Orioles pitcher Mike Mussina

whose off-the-field support of all-American causes such as milk-drinking and family literacy played perfectly into his on-field persona as baseball's hardest-working Everyman.

"He played a pretty darn important role in bringing baseball back," said Mike Flanagan, then the Orioles' pitching coach. "There's a real potential that without Cal, a lot of things would be different."

So as the roar of approval teemed over Camden Yards that night in the middle of

BASEBALL'S
25 GREATEST
MOMENTS

"The best thing about
this is that nobody is
talking about lawyers
or federal judges.
Just baseball.
Isn't it great?
We've got Cal Ripken
to thank for that . . .
I don't think we'll be
ejecting him. Short
of him shooting me
in the head, he'll be
in the game."

Home-plate umpire Larry Barnett,
before the record-breaking game

the fifth inning, Ripken, who nonchalantly trotted off the field and into the Orioles' dugout when the third out was made, stepped back out onto the grass to tip his hat to the 46,272 fans in attendance and the millions more watching on national cable television. As the ovation continued, he came out a second time, now trotting over to the seats behind home plate. He took off his hat and jersey and handed them to his wife, Kelly. Under the jersey, he wore a black T-shirt, given to him earlier in the day by his two children, Rachel and Ryan. It read, "2,130+. Hugs and Kisses for Daddy." Through the backstop, he greeted brother Billy, who played second for Baltimore in 659 of Cal's 2,131 straight games.

He went back to the dugout and put on a fresh jersey. But then came a third curtain call. And a fourth. A fifth, sixth and seventh, the crowd still roaring, the game still delayed.

"Cal wanted the game to continue," said Rafael Palmeiro, the Orioles' first baseman that night. "He wanted the game to go on. It was only the fifth inning. We'd been sitting there forever, and the fans were still cheering."

Finally, Palmeiro turned to Ripken. "You're going to have to figure something out. You're going to have to do something to get the fans settled down and get the game going again."

"Oh, no, let's just get somebody up to bat," Ripken said.

"Why don't you just go and run around and take like a victory lap or something, and see what happens?"

"No, I'm not going to do that," Ripken

Mother Vi and father Cal Sr. were front and center to help Cal Jr. celebrate the record it took him 13-plus years to break.

said. "I'm not going to do that."

Bobby Bonilla, sitting on the other side of Ripken, looked across at Palmeiro and said, "Let's just push him out there."

When they did, when Palmeiro and Bonilla physically shoved him back on to the field and toward the right-field stands, an extraordinary thing happened. Ripken, whose personality is the antithesis of ostentation, finally resigned himself to the inevitability of the adulation. He briefly embraced Orioles first-base coach Al Bumbry, who then pushed him farther toward the fans cheering him in the stands on the first base side of the stadium.

He began a long, slow, handslapping victory lap around the circumference of the playing field, communing in the moment with fans reaching over the fence to greet their hero. He slowed down to give high-fives to the Camden Yards grounds crew in right field. He paused for a few seconds to greet Elrod Hendricks, the Orioles' longtime coach, in the bullpen. He stopped for handshakes with all of the Angels, lined up in front of their dugout to congratulate him. There were words exchanged with Hall of Famer Rod Carew, an Angels coach, and with Gary DiSarcina, their shortstop, before he returned, finally, to the bench.

But the truest, most valuable message exchanged during the lap passed between Ripken and throngs of anonymous fans.

"I tried to acknowledge the celebration and acknowledge the ovation," Ripken said, "but I was trying to get the game back on line, too. And the game didn't seem to want to go back on line. So

when Bobby Bonilla and Rafael Palmeiro pushed me out of the dugout, I started the lap. The first part of the lap, I was thinking, 'OK, let me shake some hands quickly and let's get this going and then maybe we can get the game back on.'

"But as I slowly started to make my way around the stadium, I started to feel a more personal celebration. And by the time I got three-quarters of the way around, I could care less if the game started again.

"I don't remember anything that was said, specifically. It wasn't a time when you actually had verbal exchanges. There was a lot of eye contact. There was a lot of hand-shaking. It seemed like we were all communicating without the use of words. ... And I saw a few people I knew. I saw some faces I knew, but I didn't know their names. And I saw some people at the end, the guys with the Angels, I knew very well."

The lap served its purpose. After one final curtain call, the game resumed. Mark Smith, the Orioles' left fielder, stepped to the plate to face Angels pitcher Shawn Boskie. Baltimore eventually won, 4-2.

But it served its greater purpose, too. The lap was exactly what baseball needed, a symbolic, grass-roots reaching-out to its public, a gesture that took the game back to the fans rather than the other way around, rather than simply waiting and hoping and praying that the fans would come back to baseball on their own.

When Ripken, the reigning king of baseball iron men, was put on parade in downtown Baltimore, an estimated crowd of 300,000 paid its respects.

BASEBALL'S
25 GREATEST
MOMENTS

Two distinctive camera angles offer bird's-eye views of Amoros making one of the great catches in World Series history.

Johnny Podres on the mound. Dodgers leading 2-0. ... The outfield swung way around toward right. Sandy Amoros is playing way into left-center. Berra is basically a pull hitter. Here's the pitch. Berra swings and he does hit one to the opposite field, down the left field line. ... Sandy Amoros races over toward the foul line ... and he makes a sensational, running, one-handed catch! He turns, whirls, fires to Pee Wee Reese. Reese fires to Gil Hodges at first base in time to double up McDougald. And the Yankees' rally is stymied!

—MEL ALLEN, OCTOBER 4, 1955

To millions of baseball fans, it was an easy ground ball, the kind Pee Wee Reese had gobbled up hundreds of times over his 13 major league seasons. To the Brooklyn shortstop, it was the most difficult and terrifying play of his life, the final barrier between a city and its dream.

"I've heard people say they want the ball hit to them in tight situations," Reese said with a shake of his head. "They're lying."

Reese fought off the nerves, picked up Elston Howard's bouncer and fired low to first, drawing a collective gasp from the capacity crowd at Yankee Stadium. When first baseman Gil Hodges picked the throw off his shoetops, the Dodgers, the lovable Bums, the perennial bridesmaids, were champions—and Brooklyn was the center of the baseball universe. Finally.

"I remember (winning pitcher Johnny) Podres," says former Yankees shortstop

THE BOYS OF SUMMER

18

THE BOYS OF SUMMER

Robinson (right) helped the Dodgers to a six-game Series split, but he wasn't available for the Game 7 clincher because of injury.

Phil Rizzuto, recalling the final out of the 1955 World Series. "He jumped up in the air and didn't come down until all of his teammates were around to catch him. He was unbelievable."

The Game 7 script was unbelievable, replete with subplots that captured the zany flavor of Brooklyn baseball. The Dodgers had teased their always-colorful and passionate followers seven times with World Series appearances, losing five Fall Classics—all to the New York Yankees—since 1941. They had lost a National League pennant on a gut-wrenching playoff home run, another pennant on the final day of the season and a World Series game after a catcher failed to hold a third strike. But always the fans persevered and believed—and they coddled and scolded their players like family.

"Brooklyn was always the orphan borough," former pitcher Carl Erskine recalled in a 1984 interview for THE SPORTING NEWS. "We always had this problem with our identity because of Manhattan right across the river. The losing pattern of the Dodgers of the '30s didn't help. But then we all came along in the '50s to a borough that needed respectability—and we gave it to them.

"We could have won eight straight pennants when you think about it. We won in '49, '52, '53, '55 and '56 but lost out on the last day of the season in '50 and in a playoff in '51 as well as coming close in '54. All of us were in our early 20s then, just starting our families, and we were very ingrained in Brooklyn. The people there knew us as neighbors. They knew our kids' names. It was more than just a player-fan relationship. It was something genuinely deeper."

The Brooklyn-born Rizzuto, who helped feed the Dodgers' frustration as a Yankee shortstop from 1941-56, understood that personal relationship better

Longtime Dodgers Reese (left) and Hodges (right) pose with commissioner Ford Frick after helping to bring a long-awaited championship to Brooklyn.

than most.

"Brooklyn was a town that lived and died with the Dodgers," he says. "When the Dodgers were playing, you could walk up and down the streets of Brooklyn and never miss a pitch. Everybody had the game on the radio. It meant so much to them."

The city's try, try again optimism was overflowing—again—when manager Walter Alston matched Podres in the 1955 Game 7 against Tommy Byrne. The veteran Byrne had stopped the Dodgers in Game 2, giving his Yankees a two-games-to-none lead. Podres had halted the Yankees' momentum in Game 3. The 23-year-old Podres gladly embraced the pressure.

"He just felt he could beat them," recalls Jack Lang, who covered the Dodgers in 1955 for the Long Island News. "He had beaten them once before and he was a kid who had a lot of braggadocio about him. He beat them once and he thought he could beat them again."

That confidence manifested itself early. Podres blew away Yankee hitters with his hard stuff and tantalized them with a changeup that, according to Rizzuto, "made you jump out of your shoes." His teammates gave him a fourth-inning run on a single by Hodges and a sixth-inning run on Hodges' sacrifice fly. Podres carried that 2-0 lead into the bottom of the sixth, an inning that would become ingrained—along with the name Sandy Amoros—in baseball legend.

In retrospect, it seems almost fitting that

a peripheral player like Amoros, a 5-7, 170-pound Cuban with fast feet and a slow bat, would make the Series-clinching play for the Dodgers. Amoros was in left field only because Alston had pinch hit for starting second baseman Don Zimmer in the top of the sixth, forcing Jim Gilliam to move from left to second. Amoros took center stage when Billy Martin opened the Yankees' sixth by walking and Gil McDougald reached on a bunt single. The moment of truth had arrived for Podres, who now had to face lefthanded-hitting Yogi Berra.

"Yogi would either pull the ball or hit to left and Sandy was too far to left-center," Reese said after the game. "I should've been watching him, but I wasn't. When the ball was hit, I just knew it'd be in there for at least a double."

McDougald, representing the tying run, thought the same.

"Amoros was playing Yogi out by the scoreboard in left-center," McDougald recalls. "Yogi hit one of those slicing, lazy fly balls toward the (left field) foul pole. Sandy Amoros was pretty quick and he was chasing like hell trying to run it down. When he hit the track, he put on his breaks

and stopped immediately. As soon as I saw him put his breaks on, he stuck out his glove and the damn thing was there. By that time, I was halfway to third."

Amoros' great catch was only half the story. He wheeled and fired a perfect relay to Reese, who fired to first for a rally-killing double play.

"When I started out there, I looked to see where the runners were and I could see McDougald had rounded second base," Reese said. "Sandy gave me a good relay and I knew if I could get the ball to first base, I could get McDougald because I knew where he was. ... I'm sure Gil thought the same thing I thought when the ball was hit—that it was in there."

Podres thought it was going to fall and, in retrospect, he hates to consider the consequences.

"If that ball had fallen for a hit, the Dodgers might never have won a World Series in Brooklyn," Podres recalls. "Two runs were going to score and Berra might have ended up on third."

But, with the catch, any doubts about the Dodgers' ability to beat the Yankees disappeared. Destiny was smiling on the

18

THE BOYS OF SUMMER

Podres (below) was the man of the hour in the locker room and the toast of Brooklyn forever after pitching the Dodgers to a 2-0 Game 7 win over the Yankees and giving the city its first championship.

18

THE BOYS OF SUMMER

The 1955 Series started festively (right) at Yankee Stadium and ended (above) with Yankees manager Casey Stengel (left) congratulating Alston—a first-time Fall Classic winner.

Boys of Summer.

"(Amoros) was a lefthander and had his glove on the right hand," Rizzuto says. "When Yogi hit that ball, if Gilliam (a righthander) had still been out there, he wouldn't have caught it. He had to run hard toward the left field foul line and the fence. He just stuck out his hand. ..."

Alston said later he would have removed Podres and brought in Clem Labine if Amoros had not made the catch. But given the reprieve, the emotional lefty set down the Yankees in the seventh, escaped a two-on-base jam in the eighth and recorded a 1-2-3 ninth, completing his eight-hit, 2-0 shutout with the Howard ground ball that touched off a wild, wild night in Brooklyn.

"They partied all night long," Lang remembers more than four decades later. "After the game, we took a bus back to Brooklyn and it was like New Year's Eve on Times Square. The whole town just went on an all-night binge. The streets were jammed, the bars were jammed. I don't really know how to describe it. It was like the end of the world."

The New York World-Telegram compared it to another famous victory:

"Brooklyn adjusted the world championship crown on its throbbing head following the noisiest, wildest and most frenzied celebration since V-J Day in 1945. Fans clogged Fulton Street with bumper-to-bumper auto caravans. The ear-shattering din of horns, cowbells, kitchenware and cheers began at 3:45 and still sounded at midnight."

One of the grandest parties was thrown by Dodgers owner Walter O'Malley at a Brooklyn hotel and the champions were toasted in style.

"We had a huge party over at the Hotel Bossert in Brooklyn," Podres says. "It was wild. The street outside was packed, it was filled with fans. Players would go out one at a time and wave to the crowd. It was really something. The champagne was flowing. All you had to do was hold out your glass and somebody would be there to fill it up. There has never been another

Brooklyn rocked after the final out of the 1955 World Series was recorded. The first hug was delivered by catcher Campanella (39 below) to Podres and soon Ebbets Field was host for a championship lovefest, the first in its long history.

night like that in Brooklyn."

The party ended, but the exhilaration lived on in the hearts and souls of Dodger players and fans who had suffered through years—decades—of frustration in search of a World Series championship.

"After that final game, there was a big lull in our dressing room until we finally realized we had won," said former center fielder Duke Snider. "To me, it was a big thrill just seeing Pee Wee Reese so happy. There were about 50 reporters around him and he had big tears coming from his eyes. It was his first victory in six World Series. In my book, Pee Wee is the most valuable player on the Brooklyn team. In fact, he is the most valuable player they ever had or will have."

The moment was special for all the long-time Dodgers—Reese, Hodges, Roy Campanella, Carl Furillo, Erskine, Don Newcombe, Snider, Labine and Jackie Robinson, who was forced to sit out the decisive game with a foot injury. And it was easy to understand why.

"You can't imagine the hunger that existed in my belly along with the rest of the guys to win a World Series," Erskine said. "It had so much significance. There was personal pride. There was a whole city that now could raise its head, look across the river to the Bronx and Manhattan and say, 'We're No. 1.' "

Lang saw it from a similar perspective.

"They had taken so much—all those years from '47 on when they kept losing," he says. "Every time when they lost, they would have a great season in their league, but then they'd face the Yankees in the World Series. At one point I believe they felt, 'We're never going to beat these guys.' Well, they finally did."

18

THE BOYS
OF SUMMER

"I remember after
the final out everybody
was pouring champagne,
but I was sitting in front
of my locker thinking,
'Geez, we finally won.'
I didn't do any jumping
and screaming.
We had a lot of guys
who could take care
of that."

Dodgers shortstop Pee Wee Reese

One out. Batter, Adcock. Here's the pitch. There's a fly ball, deep right-center. That ball may be on through and over everything. It is gone! Home run! Absolutely fantastic!
—BOB PRINCE, MAY 26, 1959

19

HADDIX'S PERFECT LOSS

One weighed in at 170 pounds, spread thinly over a 5-foot-9 frame. The other carried 220 pounds on a powerfully built 6-4 body. When the destinies of Harvey Haddix and Joe Adcock clashed in the 13th inning of a May 26, 1959 game at Milwaukee's County Stadium, it provided a bizarre David–Goliath conclusion to one of the more amazing feats in baseball history.

The box score provides unemotional proof that Adcock, the Braves' big first baseman, got the best of that 13th-inning confrontation when he drove a pitch from the little Pittsburgh lefthander over the right-center field wall, giving Milwaukee instant victory. But baseball history salutes Haddix as the real winner that night, even

HADDIX'S
PERFECT LOSS

Braves righthander Burdette (above) was far from perfect, but he was good enough to beat the Pirates on a bittersweet night for unlucky Haddix.

in the cloak of defeat. It's hard to argue against perfection.

"It was probably the greatest game ever pitched," recalls Dick Schofield, who watched teammate Haddix pitch 12 perfect innings before suffering a gut-wrenching loss to the Braves. "Milwaukee had a heck of a team. I think anybody who played that night remembers that game as much as any game they ever played."

Nobody could have guessed that an early-season pitching duel between Haddix, an Ohio farm boy with a powerful left arm, and Milwaukee ace Lew Burdette would gain status as one of baseball's most memorable games. Pregame signs didn't point in that direction. The evening was cloudy and gloomy with rain in the forecast. And the 33-year-old Haddix, who was coming off an 8-7 season with Cin-

cinnati, was fighting the early stages of a cold, complete with sore throat.

"When I warmed up, I just didn't feel good," Haddix reported after the game. "I've been fighting off a slight cold and I just figured to do my best.

On this night, Haddix's best was not too shabby. The Braves were retired in order in the first inning. ... and the second. ... and the third. ... and the fourth. With almost mechanical efficiency, he mowed down a prolific lineup that

featured Eddie Mathews, Hank Aaron, Adcock, Wes Covington and Del Crandall.

"I pitched that game with only a fastball and a slider," Haddix said. "I threw only a few curves and a few changeups, but my fastball was jumping and my slider was great. So when I was getting them out on the two good pitches, I just kept going."

Schofield remembers another important factor: location, location, location.

"It seemed like every time I looked up at the scoreboard there were two out and an 0-2 count on the batter," Schofield says. "He had great control and his stuff was incredible that night. He just pitched the game of his life. Only a couple of balls were even hit hard. He was in total control."

Two balls hit by Milwaukee shortstop Johnny Logan were tricky. In the third inning, Schofield robbed his counterpart with a leaping catch of a line drive. In the sixth, Logan's grounder into the hole took a bad hop, but Schofield reacted to the ball, caught it with his bare hand and threw him out at first. Del Rice and Mathews backed center fielder Bill Virdon to the fence with long fly balls in the 10th.

"I think the stuff was his best, but I think control was the main thing," Virdon recalls. "He absolutely threw everything right where he wanted to. I think in the 12 innings prior to the 13th, there were not but maybe two balls hit hard. Everything was routine. I only remember one hard-hit ball to the outfield. That was a line drive directly to me. It was not a tough play."

The fifth, the sixth, the seventh and the eighth passed without incident. It was as easy as 1-2-3 for the fast-working lefty. He cruised through the ninth by striking out Andy Pafko, getting Logan on a fly to left and punching out Burdette, his eighth strikeout of the night. A perfect game—27 up, 27 down. As he walked to the dugout, 19,194 Braves fans gave him a standing ovation.

"I knew I had the no-hitter all the way because I could see the scoreboard," Haddix said. "But somewhere along the line I thought somebody had got on base.

I got a big kick out of the standing ovation from the fans in Milwaukee at the end of nine innings and I noticed my teammates were staying away from me on the bench."

Partly out of superstition, partly because of their frustration at not being able to get their pitcher a single run. The Pirates seemingly had Burdette in trouble the entire game, but Roman Mejias was thrown out at third base in a three-hit third inning, the Braves turned three double plays and fate robbed Haddix in a heart-stopping seventh inning.

"I remember a ball that (Bob) Skinner hit," Virdon says. "There was no doubt in anybody's mind that the ball was going over the fence. But in that inning, maybe at the end of the inning before, there was a storm brewing in the right field area. All of a sudden the wind came up. The storm might have blown right on by because we didn't get any rain. But that wind started blowing right prior to him hitting that ball and Aaron went back to the wall and caught the ball looking up."

Schofield remembered Skinner's near miss as well.

"Yeah, he hit a ball that was going out of the park," he says. "But somehow it just hung up there. The wind suddenly came up and stopped it."

Forced into un-charted perfect game territory, Haddix con-tinued to set down the Braves. The 10th passed quietly, so did the 11th. Haddix tired in the 12th, but still the perfect game con-tinued. Tension was high on both sides.

The scoreboard tells the story of nine perfect innings. It was a long night for Haddix, who returned to the dugout after 12 innings (below, right) with his streak still intact.

"Dick Groat was battling a slump that night and didn't play," said Haddix, who knew he had completed his 12th inning with a no-hitter, but was unsure of a perfect game. "He'd light a cigarette for me between innings, then run away without any conversation. I should have known something special was coming up but I was busy concentrating on the work at hand."

Logan, the feisty Braves shortstop who would become Haddix's teammate two

19

HADDIX'S
PERFECT LOSS

"Even today people
still remember that
game. And it makes
me very proud
that a small-town
farm boy from
South Vienna, O.,
made a little bit of
baseball history."

Harvey Haddix, 1963

Burdette (left) held the Pirates scoreless until Adcock (right) finally solved Haddix in the 13th inning.

years later, recalls the situation from a different perspective.

"He had location that day," Logan said. "He was up and down, in and out, and we hit a lot of line drives right at somebody. Unfortunately, it was his day. But we believed in winning. We had fan enthusiasm, and that kept us going. Everybody was in the game, especially the Braves because we wanted to break up that no-hitter. The fan enthusiasm got us pepped up again."

Burdette, who had recorded 37 victories while leading the Braves to consecutive N.L. pennants and a World Series championship (1957), shut down the Pirates in the top of the 13th, preserving the scoreless tie despite surrendering 12 singles. The bubble was about to burst.

Haddix faced Felix Mantilla, a second base replacement in the 11th for starter Johnny O'Brien and Milwaukee's 37th batter of the game. Haddix recalled the fateful at-bat before his death in 1994.

"Felix Mantilla led off for Milwaukee and hit a grounder to third," he said. "I can still see Don Hoak field it, look at the stitches on the ball, then calmly throw it into the dirt at first base."

Rocky Nelson failed to dig out the low throw and a hush fell over County

Stadium as the Braves recorded their first baserunner—on a perfect game-ruining error. No. 2 hitter Mathews sacrificed Mantilla to second and Haddix intentionally walked Aaron, bringing up the lumbering Adcock for a fifth time. Adcock had struck out twice and grounded out twice in his four previous at-bats.

"Adcock took the first pitch and then I got a slider a little too high," Haddix said. "He hit it well and I thought for sure it was going over the fence in right-center. When I saw the ball drop after Bill Virdon's frantic leap, I put my head down and walked toward the dugout. I thought I had lost, 3-0."

The ball barely dropped over the wire fence at the 375-foot mark, a tantalizing conclusion for a fairy tale.

"I was thinking he'd been keeping the ball away from me all night and maybe he'd do it again," Adcock said several years after the game. "And he did and I hit it."

Pirates manager Danny Murtaugh sprinted toward the downcast Haddix and draped his arm around him. "What a shame," he muttered, unaware of the bizarre developments taking place behind him on the field.

Aaron watched Mantilla sprint for the plate and, thinking Adcock's blow had

BASEBALL'S
25 GREATEST
MOMENTS

136

stayed in the park, touched second base and headed for the dugout. Adcock, running with his head down, passed second base before frantic Milwaukee coaches could pull Aaron back on the field. Aaron finally completed his disjointed tour of the bases, ahead of Adcock. Too late.

The umpires ruled Adcock had passed Aaron and awarded Milwaukee a 2-0 victory, nullifying a run. The matter was referred the next day to N.L. president Warren Giles, who changed the final score to 1-0, ruling that when Adcock passed Aaron, his potential home run became a double and only Mantilla's run counted. It was small consolation to Haddix.

"Since Mantilla scored, that was all that mattered," Haddix said. "The fact the score was changed to 1-0 didn't soothe my feelings."

And it didn't lighten the mood in the Pirates' clubhouse, where frustration had turned into guilt and remorse.

"I don't think at the moment anybody realized what an incredible feat it was, how fabulous a performance it was," Virdon said. "We were all just unhappy we couldn't score him a run. Harv was one of those guys who gave you his all and you would like to be able to reciprocate when he does something like that."

Remorse was not part of the Milwaukee post-game reaction. Far from it.

"We had a big celebration after the game," Logan said. "A lot of people said, 'Look, the guy pitched a one-hitter a lost.' Well, so what! Heck no I didn't feel bad for him. It was just one of those games where Lady Luck was on his side for being that perfect, and it just boomed out after an error."

Braves pitching coach Whit Wyatt was more pragmatic, but even he wouldn't concede to the hard-luck image that

Haddix carried for the rest of his career.

"I hated to see him lose, but I wasn't pulling for him," Wyatt said the next day. "Don't forget that Lew Burdette pitched a whale of a game. You can surely say that Haddix didn't deserve to lose, but Burdette certainly pitched well enough to win."

Burdette, an old-school, hard-line competitor like Logan, paid Haddix a special visit the day after his 12-hit shutout. Haddix recalled the meeting with a smile:

"Burdette came up to me the next day and says, 'You're a dumb pitcher.' I said, 'What do you mean?' and he says, 'I give up a bunch of little hits and you give up one big one.' "

For the record, Haddix became the first pitcher to go beyond nine innings with a perfect game. The contest lasted 2 hours, 54 minutes—the product of two fast-working pitchers who did not allow a walk until

19

HADDIX'S PERFECT LOSS

"The pressure began building up from about the third inning on. I knew I had a no-hitter. The fans wouldn't let you forget it. But the guys on our bench made me most conscious of it. They wouldn't even talk to me, not even the guys who always talk. Afraid to break the spell, I guess. And there was that big scoreboard staring at me every time I went out to the mound."

Harvey Haddix, 1959

Haddix passed Aaron intentionally in the 13th. Of the Pirates' 38 recorded putouts, infielders had 17, outfielders 13 and catcher Smoky Burgess 8. Perhaps Pirates pitcher Bob Friend, an impressed observer, summed the performance up best:

"We're happy to be teammates of a man who pitched the greatest game in history. We were breathing with him on every pitch."

If you have a lump in your throat, you're only human. ...
It's two balls, one strike on Rose. Everybody on their feet
here in Cincinnati, and a worldwide television audience
watching these moments tonight here at Riverfront
Stadium. Two-one pitch from Show. It's into left-center!
There it is! Rose has eclipsed Cobb! That's hit 4,192!

—KEN WILSON, SEPTEMBER 11, 1985

20
THE NEW HITS KING

I t's a baseball act Pete Rose has repeated thousands of times over a full-speed, run-don't-walk 23-year career. Deep, distinctive crouch, eye on the ball, patience ... patience ... patience in search of a hittable pitch. It comes, body uncoils and a line drive shoots over the infield, this time into left-center field. Cincinnati's No. 14, lights reflecting off his shiny, red helmet, aggressively rounds first base, checks the defense and retreats to the bag. Another base hit.

Only this time it's different. Fireworks suddenly fill the sky as streamers and confetti rain down on the artificial turf of Riverfront Stadium. First base coach Tommy Helms races to hug the Reds'

player/manager as other Cincinnati teammates, led by batboy Petey Rose, sprint from the dugout. The 47,237 fans stomp and roar their approval in what San Diego first baseman Steve Garvey calls the greatest ovation he has ever seen.

"Everybody's got to be someplace at some time," recalls Helms, Rose's former minor league roommate and longtime associate. "It was just nice to be in that situation. You know, I played with Pete

before we went to the big leagues, I played with him here and I came back as his coach. It was just nice to be there, to share something that I never will forget."

What Rose, Helms, the Riverfront crowd and a national television audience shared on the night of September 11, 1985, was hit No. 4,192, maybe the most anticipated single in the history of baseball. The line drive, off a 2-1 slider from Padres righthander Eric Show, moved the 44-year-old Rose past the legendary Ty Cobb, who had reigned as baseball's all-time hits leader for more than half a century. Fittingly, it came on the 57th anniversary of Cobb's final big-league game.

"I've dreamed about him," Rose had told reporters on the eve of his sprint into the record books. "There's no doubt he's the greatest hitter ever to live, based on his average. I wish I could have seen him play."

Conversely, Cobb might have

THE NEW HITS KING

Rose, left alone at first base with his thoughts (left photo), salutes the cheering fans. He finally gets a little help from his friends (right photo): Helms, son Petey and Padres first baseman Garvey.

appreciated the hell-bent style and enthusiasm Rose brought to a game the Georgia Peach had played with unprecedented vigor for 24 big-league seasons. One was a baseball demon, dedicated to the annihilation of anybody or anything that stood between him and success. The other was a baseball junkie, more personable but no less obsessed by his pursuit of excellence and victory. They were separated by time and personality, linked by drive and competitive spirit. Cobb was a human hit machine who hated to lose. Rose was a human hit machine who loved to win.

Never was that better demonstrated than on the afternoon of September 8, when Rose's Reds were scheduled to play the Cubs at Chicago's Wrigley Field. Rose, still two hits behind Cobb, was not planning to play on a rainy afternoon because the Cubs were scheduled to pitch lefthander Steve Trout in the final game of the series. Reds owner Marge Schott and Rose's wife and family had returned to Cincinnati, where the team would open a long homestand the next day. Hits 4,191 and 4,192 would be savored by the fans in the city of Pete's birth.

But the scenario suddenly changed when Rose got word that Trout had bruised his shoulder in a bicycle accident and the Reds would be facing rookie righthander Reggie Patterson instead. Rose inserted his name into the lineup and lined a first-inning single, news that did not sit well with Schott. When Rose singled again in the fifth to tie Cobb's record, Schott was not alone in her disapproval.

"He almost broke it that day in Chicago," Helms says. "We were trying to get him to take himself out of the lineup, but he almost got another hit—he hit a shot right at (shortstop Shawon) Dunston. We even got his son down to the bench to talk him into taking himself out of the game, but he wouldn't do it. That's just Pete."

Dedicated only to winning a game, Rose went hitless in his final two at-bats of a rain-shortened 5-5 tie. "I had 30,000 people yelling here and one lady (Schott)

sitting back in Cincinnati kicking her dog every time I got a hit," he quipped.

True to his season-long pattern of sitting out against lefthanders, Rose benched himself for the homestand opener against San Diego and Dave Dravecky. But a carnival atmosphere greeted the Reds September 10 when he returned to the lineup against LaMarr Hoyt. A crowd of 51,045 groaned its disappointment as an overanxious Rose went 0-for-4. But that wouldn't happen again.

"It was like people were waiting for something to happen," Helms says. "They wanted to be there, to see him get the hit. He was very professional about it. At the time, he had to handle all the media

crunch, but he always took his ground balls, always did what he needed to stay ready for the game."

Friends, former teammates and even veteran reporters still marvel at how adeptly Rose turned a long, intense media blitz into an exciting, passionate baseball event. He attacked the chase with a tunnel-vision dedication, showing up at the ballpark early and staying well beyond the end of games to cooperate with an ever-demanding and growing corps of reporters—smiling, charming, trading quips and enjoying himself as cameras, microphones and notepads recorded his every thought. It was a scenario choreo-graphed and long-anticipated by the

brash, milestone-conscious Rose, who had set his sights on Cobb years before such a pursuit became a practical reality.

And through it all Rose remained in control, an ability he had demonstrated every day of his baseball life. He was in control of his emotions, the locker room distractions, the media and the way he played the game. Nothing, it seemed, could break him down—until, that is, everybody left him standing, alone, at first base on the magical night of September 11.

After the initial round of hugs and handshakes, after Schott had run to the sideline to kiss Rose on the cheek, after a blazing red Corvette with license plate "PR 4192", a gift from Schott, had been

> "It was tremendous. I think he looked up and thought about his dad. And there was his son, to share the moment."
>
> **Reds coach Tommy Helms**

BASEBALL'S
25 GREATEST
MOMENTS

delivered, after the applause had picked back up with chants of "Pete, Pete, Pete"—everybody retreated, leaving Rose alone with his thoughts, just as he now stood alone at the top of one of baseball's most prestigious lists.

Rose looked uncomfortable as Padres players milled around and Show threw warmup pitches to catcher Bruce Bochy. He doffed his cap, waved to the crowd with his gloves and then stepped back on first and broke down. "I didn't know what to do," he said later. "I felt like a man looking for a hole to jump into. I didn't know if I was making the pitcher mad, or making Dave Parker mad because he's ready to hit."

Rose turned to Helms, threw an arm around one shoulder and put his head on the other, crying. Then Petey emerged again from the dugout, ran to his dad and the two Roses embraced.

"At first, I wiped a few tears away, then I couldn't control them," Rose said in a 1985 diary compiled for THE SPORTING NEWS. "Tommy Helms was the only one close by and I embraced him. Then my son Petey came out. I'm glad Petey came out because I needed a crutch about then."

Helms, when asked if he had ever seen such emotion from his friend, replied, "No, never." Rose, probably more than anybody in the park, was surprised by the sudden outburst.

"I can't describe my emotions because I couldn't control them after I got to first base," Rose said in the diary. "I would have been all right if the fans hadn't kept cheering for so long. When you're out there and don't have anything to do, you

After the Reds had defeated the Padres 2-0, the celebration continued with postgame tributes to baseball's new hits king, led by Cincinnati owner and superfan Schott.

start thinking about what has happened in your life and what led to everything. A lot of history went through my mind.

"Obviously, my relationship with my father was foremost. I fought (the emotion) off a couple of times. I thought about all the times he was sitting up there in the stands watching the games. I thought about the times when I was a little boy and he took me to Crosley Field."

Padres third baseman Kurt Bevacqua was caught up in the excitement.

"It was a moment without words," he said. "It's the first time I've ever seen Pete break down. As soon as the ball was hit, I was sure it was a hit. I was trying to get the cutoff throw, but (shortstop) Garry Templeton wouldn't let me have it." Templeton trotted to Rose, congratulated him and handed him the ball.

The game finally resumed after a seven-minute delay and the Reds went on to post a 2-0 victory, with Rose scoring both runs after a third-inning walk and a seventh-inning triple. After the game, he was guest of honor for a home-plate ceremony that included a congratulatory chat with President Ronald Reagan.

In retrospect, one of the things Helms remembers most about the record-breaking game was the way it ended—with Rose, baseball's newly crowned hits king, making a diving stop at first on a ground ball by Garvey. "That's just the way he was," Helms says. "He made a heck of a play to end that game. That's just Pete. I think half the people in that situation would have taken themselves out of the game. But there was Pete, still managing. That's just the way he was—he loved playing baseball."

20

THE NEW HITS KING

"I'm not the greatest hitter ever. I just have the most hits."

Reds player/manager Pete Rose

Mark Littell delivers ... High drive hit to right-center field ... it could be ... it is ... gone!
— KEITH JACKSON

Chris Chambliss has won the American League pennant for the New York Yankees. ... A thrilling, dramatic game. ... What a way for the American League season to end!
— HOWARD COSELL, OCTOBER 14, 1976

CHAMBLISS SINKS THE ROYALS

Chambliss' path to glory was not completed without a harrowing run around the bases, through a maddening crowd of souvenir-seeking Yankee fans.

I t was a boyhood dream, a home run choreographed in the back yard of every would-be baseball hero. With one mighty swing, Chris Chambliss drove a pitch into the night and began his transformation from first baseman to Yankee legend. It was a career-defining moment and instant gratification for 56,821 crazed fans at Yankee Stadium, but Chambliss would not complete his path to glory without overcoming several thousand major hurdles.

"My first thought was that I hit a home run," Chambliss says, thinking back to the 1976 American League Championship Series Game 5 finale against the Kansas

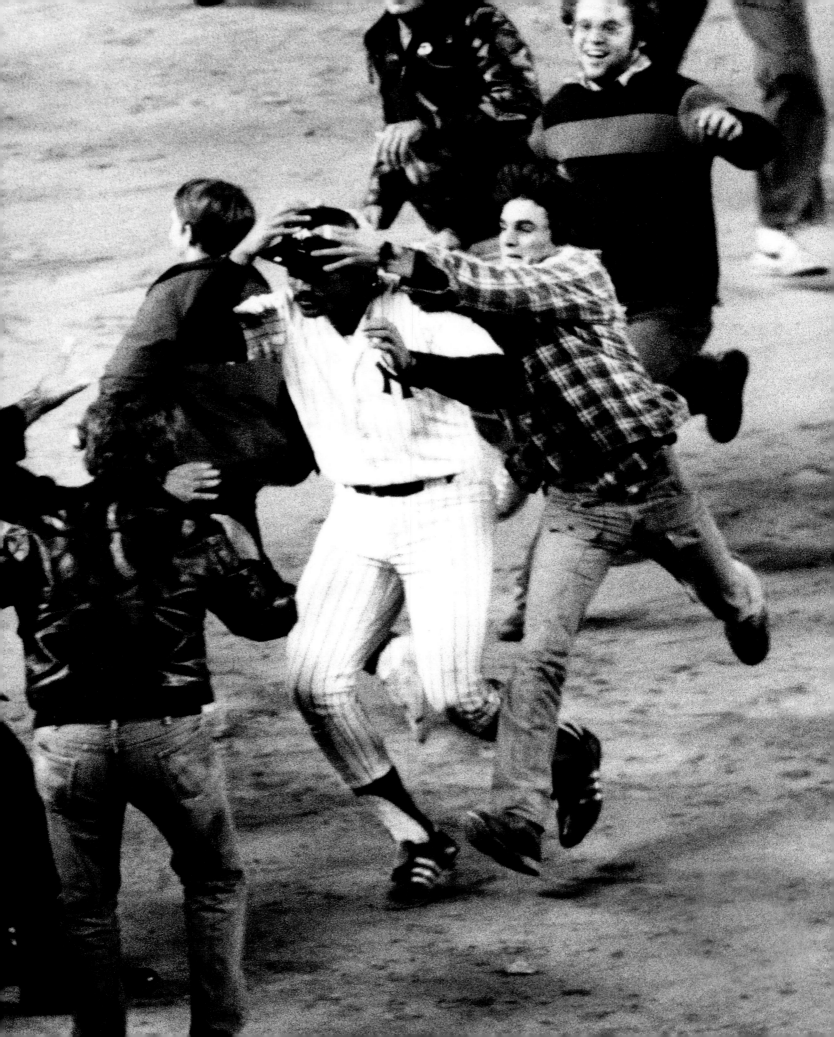

The homer (left to right): Chambliss connects and watches the flight of the ball that Royals right fielder McRae can't quite reach at the fence. Arms go up in celebration.

City Royals. "Then I realized it was the ninth inning, the game was over and we'd won the championship. Then I thought, 'Oh no, the people are on the field.' I was in the middle of a mass of people and when I fell to the ground, it was scary."

Chambliss' nightmarish home run trot started innocently enough. He watched his towering fly ball disappear over the right-center field fence, threw both arms into the air, did a little victory dance and headed for first base. As he neared second, he was already engulfed by ecstatic fans, one of whom had pulled the base from its moorings. Chambliss reached out and touched it with his hand. When he reached the spot normally occupied by the shortstop, he fell over a fan and happiness turned to concern as he struggled to regain his feet before getting trampled.

"I had gone to home plate to con-gratulate him," said Yankees third base coach Dick Howser after the game. "I saw him rounding first, then I lost him. I caught him again between second and third, but he disappeared. I figured eventually he'd make his way around if he followed the green outline."

Chambliss, bulling his way through hordes of fans, reached the spot where third base normally rested and then turned wide in a circuitous route that took him behind the catcher's box and to the dugout. Home plate was lost in a mass of humanity, but he later received a police escort to its former resting spot for a symbolic touch. The journey was complete and the Yankees, 7-6 winners, were A.L. champs for the first time since 1964.

"With the security they have now, that would never happen again," Chambliss says. "I never felt like it was fun to cele-brate that home run with the fans. They didn't belong on the field. I wanted to meet my teammates at home plate and I couldn't."

Chambliss' leadoff homer off Kansas City righthander Mark Littell brought a sudden end to a spirited playoff series against the 8-year-old expansion Royals, who had staggered down the stretch in the regular season before holding on to unseat Oakland and win their first West Division title. They didn't stagger against the A.L. East-champion Yankees, however,

winning Games 2 and 4 before jumping to a 2-0 Game 5 lead when first baseman John Mayberry homered in the first inning off Ed Figueroa.

"Here you are with a bunch of no-name guys, for the most part, finally dislodging the Oakland A's," Littell recalls. "I think we were on a roll from the very beginning. Everybody on that team pulled together. We had incredible chemistry. A bunch of no-names coming out of nowhere."

The veteran Yankees retaliated quickly, collecting three straight hits off Royals starter Dennis Leonard in the bottom of the first and forcing manager

Whitey Herzog to bring in lefthander Paul Splittorff. The game was tied after one inning, the Yankees had a 4-3 lead after three and they carried a seemingly comfortable 6-3 advantage into the eighth, with Mickey Rivers, Roy White, Thurman Munson and Chambliss doing all of the offensive damage from the top of the lineup. But the Royals weren't ready to die.

"When you're in the playoffs and the adrenaline is flowing, you never think you're dead," second baseball Frank White recalls.

Figueroa, who had settled down after the shaky first, surrendered a leadoff single to Al Cowens in the eighth and gave way to lefthander Grant Jackson, a logical move with the lefthanded-hitting George Brett (19-for-28 in his career against Figueroa) scheduled to hit third in the inning. But pinch hitter Jim Wohlford greeted Jackson with a single and Brett stunned everybody by driving a letter-high fastball into the right field seats, momentarily silencing the raucous crowd.

"When Brett hit that, it was like, 'Here we go again,' " Chambliss says. "They didn't give up, and we had gone back and forth with them all night—and all season long."

Suddenly alive and getting healthier with every pitch, the Royals carried their momentum into the fateful ninth, when the baseball gods seemed to conspire against them. The inning's first critical

21

CHAMBLISS SINKS THE ROYALS

"I thought it might be (a homer), but there's always a doubt. You know, you say to yourself you hope it won't be one of those great catches."

Yankees manager Billy Martin

21

CHAMBLISS
SINKS THE
ROYALS

moment occurred after Buck Martinez singled with two out and Cowens drew a walk off eventual winning pitcher Dick Tidrow. Left fielder Wohlford hit a slow bouncer to third baseman Graig Nettles, who fired to second for the force. Television replays showed Cowens already coming up out of his slide before the ball arrived, but umpire Joe Brinkman called him out. Instead of Brett batting with the bases loaded, the game moved into the bottom of the ninth.

"He was safe," Littell says. "Brinkman already had put up his hand. I don't know why. At that point, you're not going to win an argument. It was real obvious, but

Thousands of New York fans took the field, preventing Chambliss from actually touching home plate and even knocking him off his feet for one scary moment.

umpires are human, too. The dugout went crazy. It was very obvious to us."

White also remembers the call with a sense of what might have been. "That killed our inning big time," he says. "When you played in New York, things happened. I think the umpires felt the pressure there. (Manager) Billy Martin questioning every call put pressure on them."

Royals manager Herzog had two good reasons for not challenging Brinkman's decision.

"First, I knew they weren't going to

change the call," he said after the game. "Second, the crowd had been throwing bottles and other things all night. I was hit by a tomato during the pregame introductions. I didn't want to go out there and get killed."

That sentiment was shared by Herzog's players who, having missed a prime scoring opportunity, braced for a bottom of the ninth in which Chambliss, who would finish with an ALCS record .524 average and eight RBIs, and A.L. home run champion Nettles were scheduled to hit against Littell, a big righthander who had come on in the seventh. The hard-throwing Littell had surrendered only one home run in 104 regular-season innings.

"I had started throwing (warmups) and then I saw Mac and I stopped," recalls Littell, who was distracted by the sight of Yankee grounds crew members clearing debris from the outfield grass. The primary target of fan projectiles—"beer cans, bottles and batteries"—was right fielder Hal McRae.

"I remember Buck Martinez, who was catching, came out and I said, 'Hey, let's get off this mound. Let's get the hell off the field. Anything can happen,' " Littell says. "He said, 'They're going to get it cleared up quickly. Don't worry about it. They're already getting it pretty much cleared.' There probably was a four or five-minute delay."

During which time Littell stood and watched. After the game, even Chambliss sympathized with Littell's plight.

"It was unfortunate that people were throwing bottles," he said. "You know these people. They're crazy."

But Chambliss, sympathetic

or not, didn't take long to capitalize on the distraction.

"It was really cold that night," Littell says. "It was extremely cold. It was like these white clouds came out of nowhere and were over the stadium. And there was a pretty good gust of wind out there, which I thought was unusual. But you have to remember, it was October.

"When I threw the first pitch, a fastball, and the ball went up in the air, I thought, 'Whoa. That ball's going to come down.' But it's carrying, carrying. And the next thing I know it's out. It went out by

about 2½ feet."

As soon as the ball cleared the blue outfield wall, McRae raced for the bullpen tunnel and safety from the fans who had heckled him the entire game. Littell was too stunned to do anything in a hurry.

"I didn't know what to do," he recalls. "I just headed toward our dugout. There were so many fans coming at me, but not one touched me. I got down into the dugout and there weren't many players in there. Somebody pulled my jersey and got me out of the dugout and into the runway. All I can remember is a couple of thousand people running around going crazy."

Crazy enough to do $100,000 worth of damage to Yankee Stadium, which had to be repaired before Game 3 of the World Series against Cincinnati. Littell was led to the safety of the clubhouse, where he got a quick conference with Herzog.

"I got Mark aside and told him we wouldn't have been here if it hadn't been for what he did this year," Herzog said. "I told him to go home with his head high. I told my team to be proud of what they had done."

"What they had done" was give the heavily-favored Yankees everything they could handle in one of the most competitive ALCS ever played. But Nettles says the 1976 Yankees were never in trouble, thanks to their many offensive weapons and strong will to succeed.

"We weren't a team that relied on one guy," he says. "If Chris didn't do it, lots of other people could have. I would have been coming up later in the inning and I was the American League home run champion. It was a back-and-forth game, but we thought we were in good shape that night if we had the last at-bat with our kind of offense."

Having watched the Yankees win their first A.L. pennant in 12 years, New York fans began thinking about a more serious matter.

Check by Gossage. High drive hit deep to right field … it is gone … three-run home run by George Brett into the third tier of Yankee Stadium and Brett has taken the Royals and put them in front here in the seventh inning! The Royals now lead it, 4-2!
—AL WISK, OCTOBER 10, 1980

22 GEORGE BRETT AND THE GOOSE

The silence was eerie, a shroud of doom hanging over normally raucous Yankee Stadium. All 56,588 sets of eyes focused on the man in blue trotting defiantly around base paths that once belonged to the likes of Babe Ruth, Lou Gehrig, Joe DiMaggio and Mickey Mantle. He was an interloper on baseball's proudest tradition, a stunning dose of reality for fans in the World Series capital of the universe. George Brett had always been a thorn in the Yankees' side; now he was a nail in their coffin.

"I'll never forget the ringing sound when he hit the ball," recalls Paul Splittorff, the starting pitcher for the Kansas City Royals in Game 3 of the 1980 American League Championship Series.

Brett took center stage during the Royals' crazy ALCS-sealing celebration. A champagne-doused Brett is corraled (above) by ABC broadcaster Bob Uecker and he gets a victory hug (right) during a postgame mob scene. Home run victim Gossage (right page) was forced to contemplate a long winter.

"It just echoed through Yankee Stadium. The sound, I can still hear it today. Everyone knew it was gone as soon as he touched it off. He ran the bases and you could hear the stirring in the stands. Over the next couple of innings, you could hear a pin drop in Yankee Stadium."

Brett not only hit a home run—he delivered a moonshot into the third tier of right field seats against Goose Gossage, the most dominating relief pitcher in the major leagues. The three-run blow in the seventh inning wiped out a 2-1 Yankees lead and vaulted the expansion Royals to a playoff sweep and their first A.L. pennant after frustrating ALCS losses to the same Yankees in 1976, '77 and '78.

"It was a huge, huge hurdle for us," Splittorff says. "And we were set on doing it. We sent out our top scouts, our advance scouts, like two or three guys, to watch the Yankees. We sent them out for like two or three weeks before that playoff series. We had to get it right this time. We had lost (to them) three times. We couldn't go a fourth."

After tense five-game ALCS struggles against the Royals in 1976 and '77 and a four-game victory in 1978, the Yankees were heavy favorites to continue their mastery in 1980. The East Division-champion New Yorkers had won 103 games, six more than Kansas City had managed en route to its fourth West Division title in five years. The Yankees were gunning for a third World Series championship in four years—and New York fan expectations were high.

"The Yankees-Royals rivalry was one of the best in baseball," recalls Brett. "Last year (1998) I was working for Fox doing some commentating and they wanted to mike me and Lou Piniella. It was a Mariners-Baltimore game. So before the game, I sat in Lou's office and we talked about (the rivalry). He said it best: 'We respected you as a team, but we hated you as players. We would do anything in our power to win and you guys did the same thing.' I think that is a great way to sum up the rivalry. They had some great players, but we hated them.

"To this day, when they come (to Kansas City) or we play them in spring training, I want to beat them badly. It's nothing against the organization. You just have to remember the rivalry we had from the mid-1970s to mid-'80s and even into the '90s. It was myself, Willie Wilson, Hal McRae and Frank White going against the Reggie Jacksons, Willie Randolphs, Graig Nettles and Goose Gossages. It was a great, great rivalry. It had something to do with a small midwestern town and a big city from the East Coast."

David delivered two stunning blows to Goliath when the 1980 series opened in Kansas City. Brett, coming off a magical .390 season in which he drove in 118 runs and captured the A.L. Most Valuable Player award, set the tone with a home run that keyed a 7-2 first-game victory and his Game 2 eighth-inning relay cut down Randolph at the plate and preserved a 3-2 Kansas City win. The Yankees entered the

third game of a best-of-five series with backs planted firmly against the wall.

"I figured we'd come back to New York with at least a split," Yankees veteran Bobby Murcer said. Instead they faced quick elimination when Splittorff carried a 1-0 lead into the sixth inning of Game 3, thanks to a fifth-inning home run by White, the Royals' second baseman. But the game's complexion changed in the bottom of the sixth, when New York scored a pair of runs and significantly raised the Yankee Stadium noise level.

The flurry started with a one-out Jackson double off Splittorff and concluded with Oscar Gamble and Rick Cerone singles off reliever Dan Quisenberry, sandwiched around a throwing error by White. Yankees starter Tommy John, suddenly pitching with a 2-1

GEORGE
BRETT AND
THE GOOSE

"I think the fans in New York respected us as a team. They were never 100 percent sure if they were going to win because we had some great teams. Obviously, it was a time for them to be really concerned after someone hit a home run off their big stopper."

Royals third baseman George Brett

lead, retired the first two Royals in the seventh before Wilson slapped a lazy fly ball double down the right field line.

New York fans were understandably confident when manager Dick Howser summoned the intimidating Goose, matching his overpowering fastball against light-hitting shortstop U.L. Washington. But Washington contributed the game's pivotal play. He slapped a high chopper over the mound and beat it out for an infield hit.

"If U.L. would have run down to first at 95 percent effort or even 98 percent, he would have been out," Brett says. "But it was so characteristic of the way we played back then. U.L. was doing it like he always did. He hit the high chopper and it was a very, very close play at first. ... He enabled me to come up."

It was a matchup made in baseball heaven. Brett, baseball's premier performer in 1980, vs. Gossage, the overpowering righthander who had been virtually unhittable during August and September. "Their best hitter and our best reliever," Murcer said. Mano a mano, power vs. power.

Baseball, exactly as it was meant to be played, according to Gossage.

"George was a great hitter. I had a lot of adrenaline facing Brett," he recalls. "That was what the game was all about for me. He was the greatest hitter I ever faced.

I faced a lot of great hitters at the end of their career, but he was the best hitter I ever faced by far. He was the best hitter of the modern era.

"George, whatever you needed, he was going to get for you. He wasn't going to go for a single. He was going to try to take one in the tank. At least, that was what he tried to do with me. I tip my cap to him. It was the kind of series where it was do or die. We were two down. And we had a long way to go if we were going to come back—and it didn't happen."

Gossage went into his stretch and delivered his first pitch to Brett—a fastball down the middle.

"I remember the crack of the bat," Gossage says. "The noise. ... The noise of the bat, the sound of the bat—it was like nothing I had ever heard before. It was the loudest crack. I will never forget that crack. And then the silence."

Almost two decades later, Brett vividly remembers the challenge, his mindset as he stepped to the plate—and, of course, the picture-perfect swing.

"I moved a little closer to the plate than normal at Yankee Stadium," he says. "I figured if I got a ball middle of the plate away, I was going to try to pull it. When I faced Gossage, he didn't try to trick me with sliders. He usually came straight at me. I was thinking if I got it in the air, it could go.

"It was one of the hardest balls I hit in my life. That was probably the best swing I have ever taken in my life. To be up in a situation like that and to hit the first pitch Goose threw to me—it put us in the World Series. It was my best swing, probably my most memorable swing, and to this day it just gives me goosebumps thinking about it."

Brett's home run instantly deflated the New York crowd, but it would take more to dis-

Submariner Quisenberry, the relief ace Kansas City had been missing through its pennant drives in the 1970s, shut down the Yankees after Brett's home run.

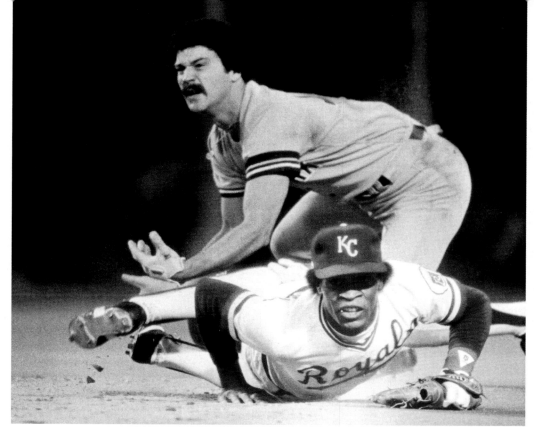

Royals shortstop Washington, pictured as he was taken out on a double-play attempt by New York's Rick Cerone, made two critical plays, one offensive and one defensive, in the Game 3 pennant clincher.

courage the veteran Yankees. As expected, they would fight back.

"It was the top of the seventh and we still had to get nine outs," Brett says. "We weren't breathing easier at all. It was still so early in the game and the Yankees were that good of a team that with three innings to go, we're thinking, 'God, this might not be enough.'"

Quisenberry, the closer Kansas City lacked in its first three ALCS battles against the Yankees, got into serious trouble in the eighth inning when Bob Watson led off with a triple and he uncharacteristically lost his control, walking Jackson and Gamble to load the bases. Quiz had a quick conversation with himself: "Hey, you know all the years the Royals had short relief problems and they blew leads—that's how they lost all those playoff games. You're they guy who is supposed to turn all that around this year. What are you walking all these guys for?"

Quisenberry went to 1-1 on Cerone, who smashed a potential game-tying line drive toward left field. But Washington stepped to his right, speared the ball and fired to second for a force on Jackson, who had broken for third. Pinch hitter Jim

Spencer grounded out to end the Yankees' final threat of the game.

"I think everybody in the ballpark thought (Cerone's drive) was in left field," Howser said after the game. "Everybody except Washington."

Brett's home run provided the margin in Kansas City's 4-2 victory, but Quisenberry's eighth-inning escape provided the exclamation point. Destiny, at last, smiled on the Royals.

"We sat there (in the dugout) and said, 'Man, it's so quiet in this place,'" recalls Splittorff. "People started leaving. By the time the ninth inning rolled around, the place was less than half full. That had never happened to us before."

A Championship Series loss had never happened to the Yankees, who had won each of their three previous playoff ventures—all against the Royals. Gossage remembers the disappointment, a failure he took personally.

"I remember crying after that game," he says. "I was in the player's lounge. I just sat there—I have always felt like I carried the weight of the team on my shoulders. That's the way I approached it. That's the way relief is. You have to have very thick skin."

> "He could just as easily have skied it, but he didn't. I knew it was out. I didn't even get up. I started thinking of who was going to pitch the next inning."
>
> **Yankees manager Dick Howser**

Casey goes into the windup, around comes the right arm, in comes the pitch. A swing by Henrich ... he swings and misses, strike three! But the ball gets away from Mickey Owen. It's rolling back to the screen. Tommy Henrich races down toward first base. He makes it safely. And the Yankees are still alive with Joe DiMaggio coming up to bat.

—MEL ALLEN, OCTOBER 5, 1941

23

THE DROPPED THIRD STRIKE

Only in Brooklyn.

It was a World Series moment choreographed for the zany, wacky New York borough, where baseballs were known to take unusual bounces and Dodgers games often confounded fans with bizarre plot twists. It was reasonable and prudent to expect the unexpected at Ebbets Field; it was wise to approach every potential victory with extreme caution.

But nobody could possibly have been prepared for the devastation that hit Brooklyn at 4:35 p.m. on a sweltering October Sunday afternoon in 1941, when sure-handed Dodgers catcher Mickey

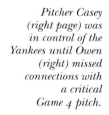

THE DROPPED
THIRD STRIKE

*Pitcher Casey
(right page) was
in control of the
Yankees until Owen
(right) missed
connections with
a critical
Game 4 pitch.*

Owen failed to catch a Hugh Casey curveball on a potential game-ending strike-out, turning a 4-3 Game 4 victory into new life for the New York Yankees. Moments later, strikeout victim Tommy Henrich came around to score the tying run and the Yankees scored three more times for a stunning 7-4 victory.

"Well, they say everything happens in Brooklyn," said Yankees center fielder Joe DiMaggio, who followed Henrich's at-bat with a single to left field. Owen's misplay would do nothing to change that

"Hugh could throw a spitter, but he didn't throw a spitter this time."

Mickey Owen

reputation.

"It was just the way we planned it," joked Yankees lefthander Lefty Gomez in an exuberant New York locker room. "We've been working on that play for months, on the quiet, you understand. And we didn't have it perfected until today."

It didn't appear early that the Yankees, gunning for their fifth World Series championship in six years, would need any miracles. They jumped to a 3-0 lead against Brooklyn ace Kirby Higbe, two of the runs scoring on a fourth-inning single

by first baseman Johnny Sturm.

It would be an uphill battle if the Dodgers, appearing in their first Fall Classic since 1920, hoped to even the Series at two games apiece. But pinch-hitter Jimmy Wasdell doubled home two runs in the fourth to ignite the Brooklyn comeback and rookie Pete Reiser gave the Dodgers their first lead an inning later when he hammered a two-run shot over the right field wall.

Enter Casey, a hulking, round-faced righthander who had suffered the loss in a 2-1 New York win in Game 3. Casey entered the game with the bases full of

Yankees in the fifth and got Joe Gordon to end the inning on a fly ball. The Yankees were helpless over the next three innings, managing only two singles and nothing resembling a threat.

"Casey had two curve balls," Owen explained in one of the many interviews he would give over the next half-century. "One broke big and broke good and then he had a hard, quick curve that looked like a slider, only it was a curve. When he came into the game that day in the fifth inning, the first two pitches I called for were the big curve, but they never broke, they just hung outside. He got away with it.

"Then he switched to the one that looked like a slider and it worked beautifully. So that's what he threw after that, the one that went down quick, and they couldn't touch it."

Casey's mastery continued in the ninth. Sturm sent a harmless grounder to Pete Coscarart at second base. One out. Red Rolfe tapped a one-hopper to Casey. Two out. Only Henrich, a lefthanded hitter with power, stood between Casey and victory.

"We had two strikes (and three balls) on Henrich with two down in the ninth," remembered Owen, who was considered one of the top defensive catchers in the game. "We were one pitch away from victory. I gave Casey the sign for a curve, and I gave him the target for a low, inside pitch."

Casey came in with a curve, but not the one Owen expected.

"Hugh rolled off the big one and I never figured he'd throw that one," Owen said. "I'm one of those guys with a one-track mind, so I was looking for the same curve he was throwing to all those other guys. I never dreamed he'd roll off that big one."

The ball broke down and in and caught Owen with his mitt in an awkward position. He was a fraction of a second late trying to stop the ball, which caromed to the right toward the Dodgers' dugout. As the home plate umpire signaled strike three, police officers jumped onto the field to discourage swarming fans. Dodgers players bounded out of the dugout in jubilation. Amid the confusion, Owen chased after a bouncing ball as Henrich sprinted toward first.

"I kept asking myself, 'How did I do it? How did I do it?' Then I made up my mind I'd have to live with it. I'd always been able to handle adversity pretty good, and I reasoned that I'd been trying my best. I've been living with it a long time now."

Dodgers catcher Mickey Owen

"With the count against me, I'm just guarding the plate," Henrich said years later. "It came in chest high, and that ball broke like no curve I'd ever seen Casey throw. As I start to swing, I think, 'No good. Hold up.' That thing broke so sharp, though, that as I tried to hold up, my mind said, 'He might have trouble with it.'

"If you take a look at the picture of it, you'll see that I'm already looking back over my shoulder. I'm expecting him to lose that ball."

The confusion was not limited to the field, where Owen was fighting his way through the police and stunned Dodgers were cutting short their premature celebration. Former Yankees shortstop Phil Rizzuto remembered his view from the New York dugout.

"I was in the dugout holding a lot of the fellas' gloves—Dimag, Henrich, Charlie Keller, my own," he said. "We didn't want to lose any of them when the game was over. When Henrich swung and missed, we all got up and started toward the runway that led out of the dugout. Some of us were already into it. I know I was.

"Then we heard all that yelling and we jumped back. There was Tommy running down to first base. Owen was chasing the ball over by his own dugout. By the time he got it, Tommy was on first and there wasn't any play."

And DiMaggio was up.

"That just goes to prove what has been said for a long time: The game isn't over until the last man is out," said Yankees manager Joe McCarthy. "It was the break of the game. They get 'em and we get 'em. They may come in the first inning or the third. Or they may come, as this one did,

"You folks and everybody else have got Mickey Owen wrong. ... We know what it means to have guys on the club who get out there and hustle. Mickey is that kind. He's always in there hustling, and there isn't a single man on our club who blamed him for missing that third strike."

Dodgers pitcher Hugh Casey

right at the finish. But, at that, it's not the break itself that counts, but what follows."

What followed was a line-drive single to left, moving Henrich to second. Keller, looking for his fourth hit of the afternoon, belted a two-strike Casey curve high off the screen atop the right field fence, barely missing a home run. Henrich scored to tie the game and DiMaggio raced aggressively around from first, giving the Yankees the lead on Keller's double. After Bill Dickey walked on a 3-2 pitch, Gordon rocketed a double off the left field wall, driving in two more runs and giving the Yankees a 7-4 lead. As Casey crumbled, Dodgers manager Leo Durocher watched impassively from the dugout and Owen never visited the mound.

"It was like a punch on the chin," said Owen, who accepted full responsibility for the Series-turning error. "You're stunned. You don't react. I should have gone out to the mound and stalled around a little. It was more my fault than Leo's."

After Yankees reliever Johnny Murphy retired the Dodgers 1-2-3 in the bottom of the ninth, the celebration began—in the wrong clubhouse.

"Boy, was that great or was it great?" Henrich shouted above the din. "What a finish! What a game! Never has there been anything like this. Never will be again, I'll bet."

The Dodgers' mood was disbelief.

"I tell you, those Yankees have got all the luck on their side," said right fielder Dixie Walker. "Never saw a team get so many breaks as they have."

"There are angels flying around those Yankees, I tell you," Wasdell said.

Casey, who would live the rest of his life as the victim of a classic misplay, talked about the 3-2 pitch calmly and without emotion after the game.

"With the count 3-and-2 on Henrich, I

figured I'd throw him a curve and put everything I had on the pitch," he said. "The ball really had a great break on it."

Spurred by their unexpected victory, the Yankees closed out the Dodgers the next day and Owen went down as one of the most infamous goats in baseball history. Over the remainder of a playing career that ended in 1954 and through his post-baseball years, he maintained a stiff upper lip, never blamed anyone but himself for the gaffe and eventually looked back at the moment with a sense of humor.

"Henrich missed (that pitch) by more than I did," Owen said. "He's the one who ought to be famous. I at least touched the ball."

Henrich struck out, but teammates (left to right) DiMaggio, Keller and Gordon struck down the Dodgers after a stunning Game 4 mistake by catcher Mickey Owen.

The pitch. … Deep to left and Downing goes back. And it's gone! Unbelievable! You're looking at one for the ages here. Astonishing! Anaheim Stadium was one strike away from turning into Fantasyland! And now the Red Sox lead, 6-5! The Red Sox get four runs in the ninth on a pair of two-run homers by Don Baylor and Dave Henderson.

—AL MICHAELS, OCTOBER 12, 1986

24 FALLEN ANGELS

Henderson (right) steps on home plate, earning a warm greeting from teammate Bill Buckner (6) and cementing his place in the Hall of Fame of dramatic baseball moments.

The aftershocks still ripple through Southern California, more than a decade after the worst baseball disaster the region has ever experienced. They come like recurring nightmares, bitter tastes that linger, bad songs that won't go away. They bring back brutal memories of a horrible October day in 1986 when a backup center fielder for the Boston Red Sox stole a pennant.

"It still hurts a lot," says Bobby Grich, who endured the pain in his 17th and final major league season. "When I go around Southern California—even around the country—and meet people, one of the first things they say to me is, 'I remember

Red Sox pitcher Roger Clemens

Henderson's dramatic ninth-inning at-bat (above) commanded the full attention of Mauch (3) and all the Angels, who felt the pain when he connected with a Moore pitch. The Angels had done the celebrating the night before, with Grich (4) and Downing leading the charge.

that game in 1986 when Dave Henderson hit that home run.' That's probably the one moment in California Angels history that fans remember more than any other.

"All the Angels fans were either at the stadium or they were listening to the game on radio or watching it on TV. Everybody knows where they were. Everybody in Southern California can remember the exact moment when Henderson hit the home run. It's something we'll never forget out here."

To fully comprehend the dramatic bombshell Henderson dropped on the Angels in Game 5 of the American League Championship Series, it's necessary to look back to Game 4. The Angels, trailing Boston ace Roger Clemens 3-0 entering the ninth inning, pulled off a miracle of their own, rallying to tie the game on a bases-loaded hit batsman and won in the 11th on Grich's one-out double. The victory gave the Angels a commanding three-games-to-one series advantage and lifted them to within one win of the first pennant in the franchise's 26-year history.

Not surprisingly, Game 5 opened amid a party atmosphere, with 64,223 fans primed for the biggest baseball celebration Anaheim Stadium had ever hosted. A two-run second-inning home run by Boston catcher Rich Gedman dulled the optimism temporarily, but catcher Bob Boone answered with a solo homer in the third and California ace Mike Witt carried his team into the bottom of the sixth inning with only a 2-1 deficit.

That's when Henderson, called into duty as a fifth-inning defensive replacement because starting center fielder Tony Armas had twisted his ankle, took center stage—in forgettable fashion.

"Something most people don't know is that I had hurt my knee in the previous game," Henderson recalls. "The right knee had torn cartilage. So I was basically just sitting there watching the game, planning when I was going to have an operation. Tony Armas went up against the wall and twisted his ankle and I was sitting there with a knee that looked as big as my head. (Manager) John McNamara looked over at me and says, 'Can you go?' I looked at the trainer and said, 'Well, let's give it a try.' So I was limping pretty bad."

Which partly explains what happened when Grich drove a sixth-inning Bruce Hurst pitch toward the 386-foot sign in left-center field with a man on base. Henderson, "limping badly," appeared to catch the ball as he jumped in front of the fence, but the ball squirted out of his glove and over the fence for a two-run homer.

"It was a surprise," Grich says. "Hurst threw me a 2-2 curveball and I was a little bit out front, and I didn't have my weight behind me—not my best power swing. But I made good, solid contact and I hit what was sort of a long fly ball to left-center. I figured it was going to be

somewhere around the warning track.

"But as I was going to first base, the ball was carrying, carrying—it got up into the jetstream. And I saw Henderson going back, back, back and I thought, 'My god, that's got a chance.' And he was right at the wall as I was rounding first base and I saw the whole thing. I saw him jump and I saw the ball hit his glove and he looked in his glove and he thought he had it. But the ball hit right in the middle of his glove and his wrist hit the fence and sort of snapped the ball out of his glove."

Grich's two-run homer gave the Angels a 3-2 advantage and it looked like it might stand up as the game-winning blow. California added two runs in the seventh, on a double by Rob Wilfong and Brian Downing's sacrifice fly, and Witt cruised into the ninth with a seemingly

comfortable 5-2 lead. It wouldn't be comfortable for long.

Bill Buckner led off the Boston ninth with a single and Don Baylor cut the advantage to 5-4 with a one-out home run. Witt retired Dwight Evans on a popup for the second out. With the lefthanded-hitting

"It still hurts a lot ... Everybody in Southern California can remember the exact moment when Henderson hit the home run. It's something we'll never forget out here."

Angels infielder
Bobby Grich

Gedman (3-for-3) scheduled next, Angels manager Gene Mauch trudged to the mound for what would become a controversial pitching change.

"Gene Mauch came out to take out Witt with Gedman coming up and I remember thinking, 'If I'm the manager, do I make the move right here?' I said to myself, 'I would definitely make the same move.' I agreed with him all the way. Gary Lucas had faced Gedman four times during the season. Gedman had struck out twice, hit a ground ball to the pitcher and a ground ball to the second baseman.

"So there's two out and Lucas hits Gedman with his first pitch. People put the blame on Mauch, but it wasn't Mauch's fault. I don't care what you say. It

24

FALLEN ANGELS

Boston third baseman Wade Boggs gets a champagne shower as teammate Baylor watches the celebration in the background.

BASEBALL'S
25 GREATEST
MOMENTS

166

"There were 64,000 people all in their starting blocks to run out on the field. ... Basically, I was looking for a way to get back to our dugout after striking out. "

Red Sox outfielder
Dave Henderson

was the right percentage move and you live or die with it, that's just the way it goes."

Mauch's next move was better received. The left-handed Lucas, having thrown one unfortunate pitch, gave way to closer Donnie Moore, a hard-throwing righthander with an outstanding forkball. Even Henderson, Boston's next hitter, agreed with Mauch's strategy.

"In those days, I was primarily a defensive replacement for Tony Armas late in the ballgame," Henderson recalls. "So I wasn't getting that many at-bats. You're looking basically at a defensive replacement who is supposed to go in there, make outs and we can go home. So

I was at a great disadvantage and Donnie Moore has a devastating forkball. Everybody talks about the pressure on me for that at-bat, but there was no pressure. Defensive replacements aren't supposed to hit closers.

"Gene Mauch caught a lot of flak for changing pitchers, but any manager would take that matchup 100 percent of the time. Donnie Moore against a defensive replacement who had five at-bats in two weeks. You gotta go with those odds. They're in the Angels' favor."

Moore came at Henderson with fastballs and quickly jumped ahead. Angels fans, within one strike of their ultimate baseball goal, were standing and howling with every pitch. California players were poised on the top step of the dugout, ready to rush the field for a joyous celebration. Everything was in place for Mauch's first World Series trip after 25 years of managing.

"There were 64,000 people all in their starting blocks to run out on the field," Henderson says. "The guards at the stadium were like 64 years old and above so I knew they had no chance of stopping these people from running out on the field. Basically, I was looking for a way to get back to our dugout after striking out."

Grich, playing first base in place of injured Wally Joyner, remembers a different kind of feeling.

"I had an uneasy feeling," he says. "I was not comfortable at all, not like game, set and match. It was a situation where I couldn't feel good until the final out was in the bag. It wasn't like I was sensing doom, but I knew what could happen. ..."

Henderson tortured the crowd and a national television audience by working the count to 2-2, then fouling off two straight fastballs. His timing was coming back. So was his confidence. "I knew I had a chance," he recalls.

Moore's third 2-2 pitch was a forkball and Henderson, slightly out in front, made

Game 5 hero Henderson was almost a goat, thanks to a long sixth-inning Grich drive that popped out of his glove and squirted over the left-center field fence for a two-run homer that gave the Angels a 3-2 lead.

Devastated but not ready to yield, the Angels fought back in the bottom of the ninth. Wilfong's one-out single tied the game at 6-6 and the Angels loaded the bases before Steve Crawford retired Doug DeCinces on a short fly ball and Grich on a soft liner to the mound.

The Red Sox missed a golden opportunity to win in the 10th, but they didn't miss an inning later when Henderson stepped to the plate again to face Moore—this time with the bases loaded. Henderson hit Moore's first pitch, a fastball, to center field for a game-deciding sacrifice fly. Calvin Schiraldi retired the Angels 1-2-3 in the bottom of the inning, sending the series back to Boston.

"It meant we were still alive and they had to put the corks back in the champagne bottles," says Boston right-hander Bob Stanley, who worked 2⅓ innings in relief and surrendered California's ninth-inning run. "I get a chill in my body when I hear Al Michaels make that (Henderson home run) call. It was almost like when the Olympic team beat the Russians. We felt like we were pretty lucky."

And pretty much in control. Right-hander Oil Can Boyd and Clemens posted 10-4 and 8-1 victories in Games 6 and 7, giving the Red Sox a World Series berth opposite the New York Mets. The Angels went home. After the Henderson home run, the bottom line was easy to read.

"When we went to the locker room after that W, the series was over," Henderson says. "And I think the Angels knew it, too."

"That baseball game was the best baseball game, the most exciting baseball game, the most competitive baseball game I've ever seen."

Red Sox manager John McNamara

solid contact with a one-handed follow-through that silenced Anaheim Stadium. The Red Sox, teetering on the edge of a cliff, suddenly had a 6-5 lead.

"There was deafening loudness before I hit the home run," says Henderson, who did a leaping pirouette out of the batter's box. "Then you could hear a pin drop after it."

Grich will never forget the devastation. "It was eerie," he says. "It was like a scene out of a movie. You have 64,000 people and there was not a whisper, it was like mute. Everybody was absolutely in shock. I think everybody was frozen in time for a few moments. It was like, 'This can't be happening.'"

Stanky is being called back from the plate and Lavagetto goes up to hit. ... Gionfriddo walks off second, Miksis off first. They're both ready to go on anything. . ... Two men out, last of the ninth ... the pitch ... swung on, there's a drive hit out toward the right field corner. Henrich is going back. He can't get it! It's off the wall for a base hit! Here comes the tying run and here comes the winning run!

—RED BARBER, OCTOBER 3, 1947

25

COOKIE CRUMBLES BEVENS

It was a matchup choreographed by the baseball gods. When New York Yankees journeyman Floyd "Bill" Bevens delivered his second pitch to aging Brooklyn reserve Harry "Cookie" Lavagetto on an October afternoon more than a half-century ago, their fates were interlocked in World Series legend. Bevens—the erratic right-hander with a big fastball and little margin for error. Lavagetto—the former Pittsburgh and Brooklyn infielder relegated to pinch-hitting duty at age 34.

Call it kismet. Chalk it up as one of those crazy ironies that color baseball's history books. But it's easy to believe there were forces beyond anybody's control working in Game 4 of the 1947 Fall Classic, when two cameo performers stepped briefly into the national spotlight and created one of the game's most enduring—and unbelievable—moments. "Don't bother writing about it," one reporter told another after the classic at Brooklyn's Ebbets Field. "Nobody will believe you anyway."

For most of the afternoon, it appeared Bevens, a 7-13 performer during the regular season and a 40-game winner over his four-year career, was not about to share the spotlight with anybody. True to his pitching style, the big kid with the 30-year-old arm was rearing back and firing—with unexpected hop on his fastball. The Dodgers, already down two games to one, could not make solid contact.

Bevens (above) was unhittable until Lavagetto (left page) connected for a dramatic two-out, ninth-inning double in Game 4 of the 1947 World Series.

Happy Brooklyn teammates and attendants escort Lavagetto (right) from Ebbets Field, moments after he had ended Bevens' World Series no-hit bid with a game-winning double.

Lavagetto, a former All-Star who was fading quickly in the final season of his 10-year career, was resigned to watching Bevens mow down Brooklyn hitters from a seat on the bench. "I was washed up," Lavagetto later admitted, thinking back to a regular season in which he batted only 69 times and collected 18 hits. His prospects of contributing anything more than moral support were slim.

Especially when the Yankees appeared on the verge of blowing the Dodgers away in the first inning. Brooklyn starter Harry Taylor failed to record an out, watching the Yanks load the bases on singles by Snuffy Stirnweiss and Tommy Henrich and a botched double-play grounder by shortstop Pee Wee Reese. When Taylor walked Joe DiMaggio to force in a run, manager Burt Shotton called in Hal

Gregg and the righthander escaped the jam without further damage. Gregg went on to work seven innings, yielding only a fourth-inning run on an RBI double by Johnny Lindell.

Bevens, staked to a 2-0 lead, was simply unhittable. But nothing would come easy on this crazy day in Brooklyn. His fastball was hopping a little too much and every inning was an adventure, thanks to the World Series-record 10 walks he would issue. He walked two Dodgers in the first inning, one each in the second and third, two in the fifth, one in the sixth and another in the seventh. Two leadoff walks in the fifth resulted in a run, thanks to a sacrifice by Brooklyn second baseman Eddie Stanky and a ground ball by Reese. But when Bevens recorded a 1-2-3 eighth inning, the stage was set for baseball's first

> "Ya know, I was sorry for that guy (Bevens). It just broke my heart right square in two when I saw those two runs crossing the plate. I just couldn't stand it."
>
> **Dodgers shortstop Pee Wee Reese**

World Series no-hitter.

"I wasn't even thinking of the no-hitter," Bevens said after the game. "I knew it was riding, but never mind about that. I'm trying to win."

The Yankees, trying to make the ninth inning easier on Bevens, loaded the bases with one out against reliever Hank Behrman. But Shotton called on relief ace Hugh Casey to face Henrich—the same matchup that had produced another magic moment six years earlier. In Game 4 of the 1941 World Series, Casey got Henrich on an apparent game-ending strikeout, only to watch catcher Mickey Owen miss the ball and set up a shocking Yankees comeback victory. This time Casey delivered one pitch and Henrich hit into a rally-killing double play.

"It was a low curveball," Casey said. "It was a perfect pitch—went right where I wanted it to go. And it

COOKIE
CRUMBLES
BEVENS

Lavagetto's double bounced off the right field wall at Ebbets Field (below), sending Yankees Bevens (left, left photo) and Joe DiMaggio into an unhappy locker room.

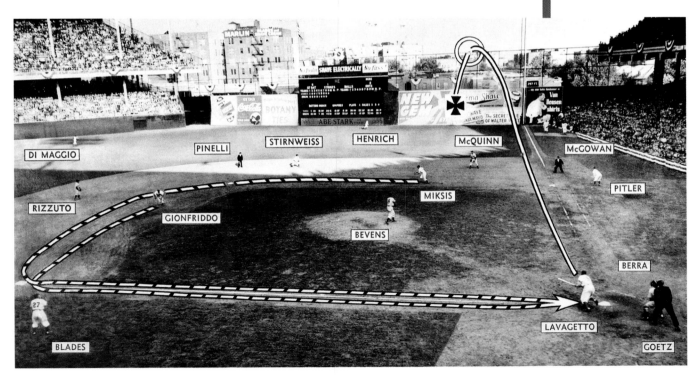

25

COOKIE CRUMBLES BEVENS

"I guess I'm famous in reverse English. People ask me what I threw Cookie, would I make the same pitch over again, did I feel Yogi should have thrown out Gionfriddo, was it right for Bucky to have ordered Reiser walked instead of letting me pitch to him, and stuff like that. What can I say?"

Yankees pitcher Bill Bevens

was a strike. What the heck: You throw it and you hope it works the way you intended it to work. That one did."

When Bevens trudged to the mound in the ninth inning, he carried a 2-1 lead and the weight of his potential accomplishment on shaky shoulders. The nervousness showed when Brooklyn catcher Bruce Edwards hit a long fly to left field that Lindell pulled off the wall for the first out. Carl Furillo was the next batter and he worked Bevens for his ninth walk. When Spider Jorgensen fouled out to first baseman George McQuinn for the second out, the fun really began.

Shotton, desperate for an offensive miracle, looked down his bench and spotted Pete Reiser, an outstanding lefthanded hitter who had severely sprained his right ankle the day before and had spent the early part of the game getting treatment in the clubhouse. Reiser could barely put pressure on his front foot and the advantage clearly belonged to Bevens. When Reiser was announced as a pinch hitter for Casey, Shotton also sent in reserve outfielder Al Gionfriddo to run for Furillo.

With a 2-1 count on Reiser, Gionfriddo shocked everybody by taking off for second.

"I slipped on the very first step," Gionfriddo said. "I thought I was a dead duck. To make up for it, when I came into second I didn't slide feet first. I just made a head-first dive for the bag. Somehow, I made it. But I still think any kind of throw would have had me."

New York catcher Yogi Berra seemed startled by Gionfriddo's dash and hesitated for a split second before making an accurate, but late, throw. Suddenly the inning had changed.

"The key to the entire inning was Gionfriddo's steal," Yankees manager Bucky Harris recalled years later. "It wasn't the fault of Bevens. It wasn't the fault of Berra, although poor Yogi got most of the blame. Actually, Berra made a sweet throw, but it was simply a case of physical impossibility. He just couldn't get the ball

there in time."

With a 3-1 count on Reiser, Harris instructed Bevens to issue his 10th walk, a move that would be roundly criticized by the New York media. Reiser limped to first and was replaced by Eddie Miksis.

"I suspect some of the boys will question my judgment in ordering that intentional pass to Reiser in the ninth and putting the winning run on base," Harris said after the game. "But I'd do it again tomorrow if I had to. You've got the tying run on second after Gionfriddo steals. The count is 3-and-1 and Reiser is a long-ball hitter. I'm not going to give him a chance to whack one over the fence. I suppose it is against baseball legend to order that pass, but the second guess is always the best one, and I get only one."

Again Shotton rolled the dice and this time he came up with Lavagetto, who was surprised to get the call against a right-handed pitcher. But Shotton had used Arky Vaughan earlier and was out of left-handed swingers.

"Sure, I realized Bevens was working on a no-hitter when I was called off the bench to pinch hit for Stanky," Lavagetto said. "But that didn't make any difference. It was my bread and butter or his. He slipped over a strike on me with his first pitch."

Lavagetto took a big swing and missed, bringing Bevens to within two strikes of immortality. But pitch No. 2—a fastball high and outside—met with a different fate.

"My next pitch was just where I wanted it," Bevens said. "The pitch was high and away. Fast and outside were the printed instructions for Lavagetto and fast and outside was what he got."

Lavagetto disagreed with the Yankee scouting report. "If they were pitching fast and outside to me, they were almost exactly wrong. Fast and tight was the way to handle me. I thought Bill tried to pitch inside to me and the ball got away from him."

Lavagetto reached out and shot a drive toward the right field wall at cozy Ebbets Field. A hush fell over the capacity crowd as right fielder Henrich, stationed in right-

COOKIE
CRUMBLES
BEVENS

*Lavagetto (left)
might have felt sorry
for Bevens (right),
but that didn't keep
him from enjoying
the fruits of his
defining career
moment.*

center, made a mad dash to cut it off. He couldn't and the ball hit the barrier, struck Henrich on the shoulder and bounded away. Gionfriddo and Miksis dashed home, ending both the no-hitter and Bevens' hope for victory. Not only had the Dodgers recorded an unlikely 3-2 win, they had knotted the Series at two games apiece.

"As soon as the ball was hit, I ran to back up home plate," Bevens said. "When Miksis slid across the plate almost on Gionfriddo's heels, I saw umpire Larry Goetz move up to brush off the plate. He was so wrapped up in the game, he didn't even know it was over. But I sure did."

Pandemonium gripped Ebbets as excited Dodgers carried Lavagetto on their shoulders and ecstatic fans rushed the field. Stunned Yankees walked dejectedly to their clubhouse.

"It was losing the game that hurt, not losing the no-hitter," Bevens insisted. "I

walked 10 and to me a walk is as bad as a base hit. You don't deserve to win when you walk that many."

The Dodgers' celebration was short-lived. The Yankees roared back for a 2-1 Game 5 victory behind Spec Shea, who struck out pinch hitter Lavagetto in the ninth with the tying run on base. The Yankees would win the 1947 Series in seven games and neither Lavagetto nor Bevens would appear in another major league contest. Years later, Lavagetto made a confession about his moment in the spotlight.

"I felt kind of sorry for Bevens," he said. "I told him so the next day when the photographers posed us for our picture together. 'It's all right, Harry,' he said. 'That's baseball.' But he must have been still choked up over what had happened. One pitch and I was the hero and he was the goat—that's sure baseball."

1 Merkle mistake costs Giants—1908

New York first baseman Fred Merkle became baseball's biggest goat when he failed to touch second base on an apparent game-winning hit by teammate Al Bridwell, a mistake that would cost the Giants a pennant. When the Cubs appealed by touching second, Merkle was called out and umpire Hank O'Day declared the game a 1-1 tie. The teams finished the season with identical records and the Cubs won a makeup game—and the pennant.

2 Aging Alexander rescues Cardinals—1926

In one of the most memorable matchups in baseball history, 39-year-old Grover Alexander fired a seventh-inning third strike past young Yankee slugger Tony Lazzeri with the bases loaded in a tense World Series Game 7. Alexander, who had pitched a complete-game victory the day before, went on to blank the Yankees over the final two innings of a 3-2 Series-deciding win.

3 DiMaggio's streak ends in Cleveland—1941

Cleveland shortstop Lou Boudreau grabbed a bouncer up the middle, stepped on second and threw to first for an eighth-inning double play—the play that officially ended the record 56-game hitting streak of New York center fielder Joe DiMaggio. Before the double play, DiMaggio had bounced out twice to third baseman Ken Keltner and walked in a game won by the Yankees, 4-3, at Cleveland Stadium.

4 Ruth's 60th homer beats Senators—1927

The incomparable Babe Ruth stroked a 1-1 pitch from Washington lefty Tom Zachary into the right field stands at Yankee Stadium for his 60th home run, breaking the single-season record he had set in 1921 and tied one day earlier. The two-run shot, Ruth's 17th homer in September, broke a 2-2 tie in the eighth inning and sparked the Yankees to a 4-2 victory.

5 Williams finishes season at .406—1941

Ted Williams, who refused to sit out a final-day doubleheader with a .39955 batting average, concluded a six-hit outburst with a 2-for-3 nightcap performance that lifted his final average to .406—the first .400 average in baseball since 1930. Williams finished the doubleheader with six hits in eight at-bats.

6 Hartnett helps Cubs see the light—1938

Chicago manager/catcher Gabby Hartnett drilled a two-out, two-strike, ninth-inning home run into the thickening gloom at Wrigley Field, giving his pennant-contending Cubs an important 6-5 win over Pittsburgh just as umpires were ready to call the game a tie because of darkness. Many of the 34,465 Cubs fans had to strain to see the ball, hit off Pirates pitcher Mace Brown, disappear over the left field wall.

7 Vander Meer pitches 2nd no-hitter—1938

Cincinnati lefty Johnny Vander Meer retired Brooklyn's Leo Durocher on a fly ball with the bases loaded, completing his 6-0 victory and record second straight no-hitter. Vander Meer, who had no-hit the Boston Bees, 3-0, five days earlier, matched that feat at Ebbets Field in Brooklyn's first game under lights—the first major league night game outside Cincinnati.

8 Bad-hop grounder lifts Washington—1924

The Washington Senators, long the doormat of the American League, captured their first World Series when two routine Game 7 ground balls inexplicably hopped over the head of New York third baseman Fred Lindstrom,

producing three runs. The Senators tied the game 3-3 in the eighth inning on manager Bucky Harris' two-run, bad-hop single and clinched their championship in the 12th when Earl McNeely's bouncer hopped high over Lindstrom's head, producing a 4-3 win.

9 Smith shocks Dodgers with bat—1985

St. Louis shortstop Ozzie Smith, the Wizard of Oz known for his outstanding glovework, stunned a capacity crowd at Busch Stadium by hitting a ninth-inning home run off Los Angeles closer Tom Niedenfuer to give the Cardinals a 3-2 victory in pivotal Game 5 of the National League Championship Series. The shot over the right field wall was the first lefthanded home run in the eight-year career of the switch-hitting shortstop.

10 Puckett takes center stage—1991

Minnesota center fielder Kirby Puckett drilled a solo home run in the 11th inning off Atlanta lefty Charlie Leibrandt, giving the Twins a 4-3 victory and forcing a Game 7 in the World Series. The dramatic home run was icing on the cake for Puckett, who had driven in two earlier runs with a triple and a sacrifice fly and made an outstanding leaping catch to rob Braves outfielder Ron Gant.

OTHER GREAT MOMENTS:
THE ALL-STAR GAME

3 Rose crunches Fosse, gives N.L. win——1970

Pete Rose thrilled his hometown Cincinnati fans when he raced around from second base on a 12th-inning single by Chicago's Jim Hickman and bowled over Indians catcher Ray Fosse while scoring the winning run in a violent, but dramatic, end to a 6-5 N.L. victory.

4 Reggie Jackson drops a bomb on N.L.——1971

Young Oakland slugger Jackson drove a third-inning pitch from Pittsburgh's Dock Ellis high off a light tower on the roof at Detroit's Tiger Stadium, a mammoth drive that traveled 520 feet. The two-run shot, one of three A.L. homers, keyed a 6-4 victory that ended an eight-game A.L. losing streak.

5 Fred Lynn slams N.L.'s 11-game jinx——1983

California center fielder Lynn capped a seven-run third inning with the first grand slam in All-Star Game history and propelled the A.L. to a 13-3 victory. The win ended the league's embarrassing 11-game losing streak.

6 Williams shines in easy A.L. victory——1946

Boston's Williams capped a four-hit, five-RBI show when he hit his second home run, an eighth-inning shot off the famed "ephus" pitch of Pittsburgh's Rip Sewell that delighted his home fans in a 12-0 A.L. win at Fenway Park.

1 Carl Hubbell strikes out five straight——1934

Starting for the N.L. before his home fans at New York's Polo Grounds, Giants lefty Hubbell recorded consecutive strikeouts of Yankee sluggers Babe Ruth and Lou Gehrig, Philadelphia's Jimmie Foxx, Chicago's Al Simmons and Washington's Joe Cronin in the first and second innings of baseball's second midsummer classic.

2 Ted Williams has a blast in A.L. victory——1941

Boston slugger Williams, given a chance to bat when N.L. second baseman Billy Herman made a poor relay throw to first on what should have been a game-ending double play, hit a dramatic two-out, three-run homer in the bottom of the ninth inning to give the A.L. a 7-5 victory in a game at Detroit's Briggs Stadium.

9 Williams' appearance steals show—1999

Hall of Famer Williams, 80 years old and driven onto the field in a golf cart, stood up long enough to throw the ceremonial first pitch of the All-Star Game before being surrounded by current players and friends in an emotional and touching moment at Fenway Park, his baseball home for 19 spectacular major league seasons. Williams spent several minutes laughing and talking with admiring players before watching the A.L. record a 4-1 victory.

10 Tony Perez catches Catfish—1967

Cincinnati's Perez, a replacement for Dick Allen at third base, belted a 15th-inning pitch from Oakland righthander Catfish Hunter over the left field fence, giving the N.L. a 2-1 win in the longest midsummer classic in the 35-year history of the event. Perez's one-out homer ended a masterful game that was dominated by a combined 12 pitchers. Ironically, Philadelphia's Allen had homered in the second inning for the only other N.L. run.

7 Musial ends classic in 12th inning—1955

Cardinals slugger Stan Musial hit the first pitch he saw in the bottom of the 12th inning off Boston's Frank Sullivan for a game-winning homer as the N.L. posted a come-from-behind 6-5 victory at Milwaukee's County Stadium.

8 Callison rescues N.L. with home run—1964

Philadelphia's Johnny Callison pounded the first pitch he saw from Boston relief ace Dick Radatz over the right field fence with two out and two men on base in the ninth inning, giving the N.L. a stunning 7-4 win at New York's Shea Stadium.

OTHER GREAT MOMENTS:
MOMENTS THAT CHANGED THE GAME

3 Pirates, Red Sox play first Series—1903

The venerable Cy Young, the ace of Boston's staff and winningest pitcher in baseball history, drew the honor of firing the first World Series pitch to Pittsburgh center fielder Ginger Beaumont. The Pirates beat Young in the inaugural, but the Red Sox rebounded to win the first Series in eight games.

4 Baseball's first 'Game of Century'—1933

New York's Lefty Gomez threw the first pitch to Cardinals infielder Pepper Martin in what was billed as baseball's Game of the Century at Chicago's Comiskey Park. The first All-Star Game, conceived by Chicago sportswriter Arch Ward, was won by the American League, 4-2, thanks to a two-run, third-inning homer by Yankee great Babe Ruth.

5 Astrodome ushers in new era—1965

Houston's Bob Bruce fired the first regular-season pitch in the new Astrodome, officially introducing indoor baseball to the major leagues. The Phillies ruined the festive occasion by recording a 2-0 victory behind lefty Chris Short.

1 Jackie Robinson breaks color barrier—1947

With the first pitch of the 1947 season by Brooklyn's Joe Hatten, Robinson took his place in history as the first black major league player in more than six decades. The 28-year-old Robinson, who broke the color barrier in the Dodgers' 5-3 opening day victory over Boston, played first base and went 0-for-3 off Johnny Sain, although he did reach base on an error and scored the winning run.

2 Baseball lights up in Cincinnati—1935

When President Franklin D. Roosevelt pressed a button hundreds of miles away in Washington D.C., Cincinnati's Crosley Field transformed into a glowing wonderland and fans officially welcomed night baseball and a new era for the National Pastime. Under the watchful eye of Cincinnati G.M. and innovator Lee MacPhail, the Reds recorded a 2-1 victory over the Phillies.

6 Giants win West Coast inaugural—1958

Giants starter Ruben Gomez threw the first pitch in the inaugural major league game on the West Coast and then went on to shut out the Los Angeles Dodgers, 8-0, on a history-making afternoon at San

Francisco's Seals Stadium. The game marked the West Coast debut for both the Giants, transplanted from New York, and the Dodgers, former tenants of Brooklyn.

7 Frank Robinson makes history—1975

Frank Robinson, making his historic debut as baseball's first black manager, spiced his emotional afternoon with a first-inning home run in his part-time role as designated hitter and went on to guide his Cleveland Indians to a 5-3 opening day win over New York at Cleveland Stadium.

8 Major league baseball is on the air—1939

With Red Barber handling play-by-play for NBC affiliate W2XBS, an experimental station in New York, major league baseball made its television debut with the airing of Cincinnati's 5-2 win over the Dodgers in a doubleheader opener at Brooklyn's Ebbets Field.

9 Interleague play begins at Texas—1997

Texas lefty Darren Oliver made baseball history when he fired the first pitch to San Francisco's Darryl Hamilton in the first interleague game of the modern era at The Ballpark in Arlington. The Giants won the history-making battle, 4-3.

10 Blomberg becomes first DH—1973

The great designated hitter experiment became an American League reality when New York's Ron

Blomberg stepped to the plate in the first inning of an opening day game against Boston at Fenway Park. Blomberg drew a bases-loaded walk off Red Sox starter Luis Tiant.

OTHER GREAT MOMENTS:
UNUSUAL, AND UNFORGETTABLE

1 Short promotion amuses Browns fans—1951

St. Louis Browns owner Bill Veeck shocked the baseball world when he signed midget Eddie Gaedel and sent him to the plate in the first inning of the nightcap of a doubleheader against Detroit. Gaedel, wearing uniform No. $1/8$, walked on four pitches, trotted to first and left for a pinch runner.

2 Too much pine tar, umpires rule—1983

George Brett's two-run, ninth-inning homer off Goose Gossage, apparently giving Kansas City a 5-4 win at Yankee Stadium, was wiped out by umpires who ruled he had too much pine tar on his bat, thus making it illegal. Brett's tirade was recorded for posterity and officials eventually overruled the decision, resulting in a Royals' victory.

3 Rick Monday rescues the flag—1976

Chicago Cubs center fielder Rick Monday made a dramatic catch when he dashed into left field at Dodger Stadium and snatched an American flag away from two protesters, who were trying to set it on fire. The patriotic Monday earned a standing ovation from 25,167 appreciative Los Angeles fans and became a national celebrity in baseball's Bicentennial season.

4 Yanks win, with help from a friend—1996

Jeff Maier, a 12-year-old fan at Yankee Stadium, stuck his glove over the right field fence and pulled in a long drive by Yankee shortstop Derek Jeter, a ball that might have been caught by Baltimore outfielder Tony Tarasco. The controversial play was ruled a home run and the Yankees went on to record a 5-4 win in the opener of the ALCS.

5 Marichal attacks Roseboro—1965

Juan Marichal, thinking Dodgers catcher John Roseboro had whizzed a return throw too close to his ear, turned around and attacked him with a bat, touching off a 14-minute brawl that shocked 42,807 fans at Candlestick Park.

7 Earthquake interrupts World Series—1989

Just moments before the start of World Series Game 3 between San Francisco and Oakland, an earthquake measuring 7.1 on the Richter scale rocked Candlestick Park, a phenomenon that caused

Terry Pendleton's eighth-inning double had been caught and failed to score, a baserunning gaffe that spiced up a Game 7 eventually won by the Twins in 10 innings, 1-0.

9 Idle Ripken steals the spotlight—1998

This memorable moment was precipitated by a man who decided *not* to play in a game. Baltimore third baseman Cal Ripken unexpectedly announced before the Orioles' final home contest of the season that he would sit out and end his record consecutive-games streak at 2,632. The Yankees' 5-4 victory was lost in the shadow of the historic moment.

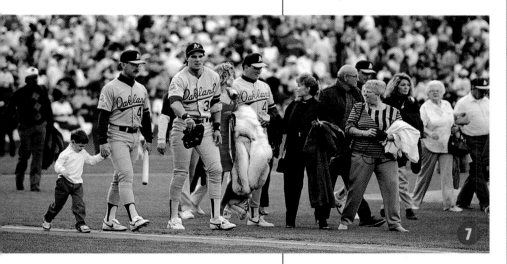

6 Disco Demolition Night goes awry—1979

White Sox owner Bill Veeck watched helplessly as his Disco Demolition Night promotion turned into an out-of-control bonfire and riotous romp for unruly fans at Comiskey Park, forcing the White Sox to forfeit the second game of a doubleheader against Detroit.

death and destruction in the Bay Area and forced postponement of the classic for an unprecedented 10 days.

8 Lonnie Smith freezes and Braves lose—1991

Smith might have cost Atlanta a World Series when he was duped by Minnesota infielders into thinking

10 Denkinger says safe, Cards boil—1985

A safe call by A.L. umpire Don Denkinger lives in infamy in St. Louis. When Jorge Orta was ruled safe at first base (replays showed he was out) leading off the ninth inning of World Series Game 6, Cardinals players and manager Whitey Herzog argued vehemently. The Royals went on to score two runs and claimed a 2-1 victory and then captured their first title the next night with an 11-0 win over the still-fuming Cardinals.

OTHER GREAT MOMENTS:
INDIVIDUAL FEATS

1 Wambsganss triples his pleasure—1920

The 1920 World Series, a seven-game Cleveland victory over Brooklyn, was spiced by the only unassisted triple play in postseason history. It was pulled off in the fifth inning by Indians second baseman Bill Wambsganss, who caught a Clarence Mitchell line drive headed for center field, stepped on second to double Pete Kilduff and wheeled around to tag Otto Miller, who had strayed too far off first base.

2 Tigers rally, give McLain 30th victory—1968

Willie Horton's one-out, ninth-inning single over a drawn-in outfield scored Mickey Stanley and gave Detroit a 5-4 victory over Oakland and Denny McLain the distinction of becoming baseball's first 30-game winner in 34 years. McLain, 31-6, became the first to reach that lofty plateau since Dizzy Dean won 30 games for the St. Louis Cardinals in 1934.

3 Henderson steals record from Brock—1982

Oakland left fielder Rickey Henderson swiped second base in the third inning of a game at Milwaukee and claimed baseball's single-season basestealing record, moving past former Cardinals great Lou Brock. Henderson's record 119th steal came on a pitchout by Brewers righthander Doc Medich and the speedy A's star went on to steal three more bases in the game en route to his record final season total of 130.

4 Ruth's 'called shot' deflates Cubs—1932

With one big arm-sweeping motion toward center field, Yankee great Babe Ruth added a memorable page to baseball legend. Ruth, responding to taunts from the Cubs dugout during World Series Game 3 at Chicago's Wrigley Field, made his gesture and then hit Charlie Root's 2-2 pitch over the center field fence—his second home run of the game. Whether Ruth was calling his shot or simply motioning to the Cubs bench, nobody knows for sure. But the homer remains one of the most famous in baseball history.

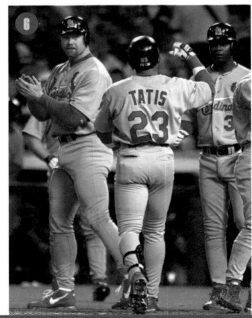

5 Tigers get a big whiff of Gibson—1968

St. Louis Cardinals ace Bob Gibson, following up on a phenomenal regular season in which he compiled a 1.12 ERA, fired a called third strike past Detroit slugger Willie Horton to complete a dominating 4-0 Game 1 shutout that featured a World Series-record 17 strikeouts.

6 Tatis gives double slam to Dodgers—1999

St. Louis third baseman Fernando Tatis became the first player in history to hit two grand slams in one inning when he drilled a 3-1 pitch from Chan Ho Park over the left-center field fence to cap an 11-run Cardinals outburst at Dodger Stadium. Park, a righthander, was the victim for both home runs.

7 Ryan gets 5,000th strikeout—1989

Rubber-armed Nolan Ryan, the Texas Rangers' 42-year-old bionic man, became the first pitcher in history to record 5,000 career strikeouts when he fired a 96-mph fastball past Oakland's Rickey Henderson to the delight of 42,869 fans at Arlington Stadium.

8 Garber fans Rose, ends hitting streak—1978

Cincinnati third baseman Pete Rose, batting in the ninth inning of

a game Atlanta led 16-4, swung and missed a Gene Garber changeup for strike three, ending his National League-record tying hitting streak at 44 games. Rose finished the game at Atlanta's Fulton County Stadium hitless in five at-bats.

9 Whiten ties two records in one game—1993

St. Louis outfielder Mark Whiten joined two elite clubs when he became the 12th player to hit four homers in a game and the second to drive in 12 runs in a game. Whiten's two-run, ninth-

inning homer capped a 15-2 Cardinals' win in the nightcap of a doubleheader at Cincinnati.

10 Clemens strikes out 20 again—1996

Boston righthander Roger Clemens, matching the single-game record he had set more than 10 years earlier, got Travis Fryman for his 20th strikeout in a dominating 4-0 victory over the Detroit Tigers at Tiger Stadium. Clemens struck out every batter in Detroit's starting lineup and got third baseman Fryman four times.

Photo Credits

T = Top B = Bottom L = Left R = Right M = Middle C = Center

The Sporting News Archives—Cover, 9 (6), 12, 13, 14-15, 16 T, 18, 19 (2), 20-21, 24 (3), 25 (2), 27 T, 30 (2), 32 T, 33, 56, 60, 63, 70, 71, 72-73, 74, 75 B, 76, 78-79, 80, 81, 82, 83, 88 (3), 92, 93, 94 (L, R), 95, 105, 106T, 107 R, 108 T, 109 T, 109 R, 110, 114, 115 (2), 124, 125, 126 T, 127, 128, 129, 130 (2), 132-133, 134, 135 (3), 136, 137, 142, 158, 159, 160, 161, 170, 171 B, 173, 174, 175, 176, 178, 179 T, 179 M, 180, 181 B, 182 T, 183 R.

AP/Wide World Photos—10-11, 16 B, 31, 34 L, 34 R, 35, 36 R, 40, 41, 42 (3), 44, 46, 50, 51, 63, 75, 94, 98, 100, 101, 104, 107 T, 140, 144-145, 146 R, 148 R, 149 L, 156-157, 168, 169, 171 T, 175 B, 179 L, 181 T, 182 B, 183 L.

UPI/Corbis Bettmann—6-7, 9 TM, 9 RM, 17, 23, 28-29, 30T, 34 T, 36 L, 38 (2), 39, 42 (2), 45, 65 (2), 68 (2), 69 (3), 45, 47 B, 84-85, 102, 106 L, 131, 135, 139, 150, 164 B, 165, 166, 167, 177, 180 B.

Reuters/Corbis Bettmann—111, 112 R.

Albert Dickson/The Sporting News—Cover (2), 54, 55, 57, 118 (2), 119, 120-121, 122, 123 (2), 177 B.

Dilip Vishwanat/The Sporting News—59 B, 77.

Robert Seale/The Sporting News—52-53, 58, 59 T.

Bob Leverone/The Sporting News—58.

Boston Globe—62, 90 L, 99, 100 (2), 103.

Vincent Riehl/New York Daily News—146 L, 147 R, 148.

Dan Farrell/New York Daily News—88 R.

Dick Lewis/New York Daily News—86.

Gene Kappock/New York Daily News—147 T, 149 R.

Harry Hamburg/New York Daily News—91.

New York Daily News—67.

John Spink/Kansas City Star—155.

Louis Requena—179 R.

Mitchell Layton—154.

Karl Merton Ferron/Baltimore Sun—116, 184-185.

Malcolm Emmons—9 C, 96.

George Silk/Life Magazine—26 B.

Tony Tomsic/Sports Illustrated—141, 143.

Neil Leifer/Sports Illustrated—43, 87.

Heinz Kluetmeier/Sports Illustrated—48, 49, 88 L, 89, 90 T, 152.

Tony Triolo/Sports Illustrated—36, 37.

Richard Mackson/Sports Illustrated—163, 164.

Walter Iooss Jr./Sports Illustrated—153.

George Tiedemann/Sports Illustrated—47 T.

John Iacono/Sports Illustrated—64.

Mark Kauffman/Sports Illustrated—126 L.

Marvin Newman/Sports Illustrated—22.

Ron Vesely/Major League Baseball—112 L, 113.

Michael Zagaris/Major League Baseball—112 TL.

Rick Labranche/ESPN—6.

United Media—97.